THE COLLEGE BOARD

THE

COLLEGE

BOARD

ITS FIRST FIFTY YEARS

By Claude M. Fuess

NEW YORK

College Entrance Examination Board

1967

First printing 1950
Second printing 1967

Manufactured in the United States of America

PREFACE

NOBODY REALIZES more fully than I that a book about
the College Entrance Examination Board is unlikely
to rival the works of Conan Doyle or John P. Mar-
quand as a "best-seller" or to bring its author either
fame or fortune. On the other hand, I have seen enough
of the Board, as schoolmaster and member, to believe
that its story is an important phase of educational evolution in the United States. Its leaders have been leaders also in colleges and schools, and their thinking has
been constructive. The Board itself, whatever its future
may be, has already made an important contribution,
and its development, even though unromantic, is worth
recording.

Although the material for this book has been found
largely in the published reports of the Board and its
committees, I have also consulted the correspondence of
President Charles W. Eliot, President Nicholas Mur-
ray Butler, and Dr. Wilson Farrand relative to its
origins. I have had the advantage, too, of talking with
Dr. Frederick C. Ferry, Dr. Radcliffe Heermance,
Dr. Richard M. Gummere, Dr. Edward S. Noyes, Miss
Myra McLean, Dean Margaret T. Corwin, Mr. Allan
R. Blackmer, Mr. Henry Chauncey, Mr. William C.
Fels, and others. I owe a special debt to Mr. Frank H.

Bowles, the present Director, and his associates at the Board headquarters for many courtesies extended to me, and above all to my friend, Professor George W. Mullins, who has read the manuscript, answered questions patiently, and proved to be a mine of information. My personal memory of the Board and its meetings goes back to the 1920's when I first began serving on its committees, and over the years I have been intimately associated with a large number of the members.

I have tried to give credit for all quoted statements from representatives of the Board. Whatever opinions are expressed here and there in the text are my own, and nobody else should be blamed for them.

What seemed at first like rather a dull task has proved to be a pleasant excursion into the past. I can only hope that I have been able in some degree to revive and portray the men and women who have been an inspiration to so many teachers of a younger generation.

CLAUDE M. FUESS

Chestnut Hill
Massachusetts
January 1, 1950

CONTENTS

THE COLLEGE BOARD

CHAPTER I

BIRTH OF AN
IDEA

The College Entrance Examination Board was in its origins an attempt to introduce law and order into an educational anarchy which towards the close of the nineteenth century had become exasperating, indeed almost intolerable, to schoolmasters. The basic trouble lay in a lack of co-operation among colleges as a group and between colleges and secondary schools on the matter of college admissions. The solution reached seems in retrospect so wise and inevitable that it is difficult to comprehend why it was not accomplished earlier or why it met with any resistance. But education has always been wedded to tradition. Because college faculties are usually strongholds of conservatism, their response to new ideas is seldom spontaneously enthusiastic. Nobody admits this more readily than educators themselves, who are often individually and collectively timid, fearful that change may mean disaster, and preferring to bear those ills they have than fly to others that they know not of. This is why it frequently takes a crisis to clear the air and expedite a reform.

Such a crisis did exist in the 1890's, when each separate college insisted on prescribing its own standards for admission to its Freshman Class, regardless of what other institutions were doing or of the embarrassment caused to preparatory schools and, indeed, to the general public for whose benefit educational institutions were presumably designed. They just could not agree. While most of those in authority were aware of what was needed, they were in doubt as to the most efficient means of securing it—like the American colonies groping towards unity in the 1780's or the world before the United Nations. It took competent and confident guidance, blessed with patience, persistence, and tact, to lead the colleges from perfunctory and futile discussion to intelligent planning. The idea had to be lodged and then to permeate and had to triumph over inertia, smugness, prejudice, and suspicion. The creation and growth of the College Entrance Examination Board against such obstacles have accurately been described by Julius Sachs as "epoch-making in the history of American secondary education."

Before 1800, apparently, only Greek, Latin, and Arithmetic were required for admission to college, and a commendable degree of articulation existed between colleges and schools. Most candidates for college were trained under similar conditions in classical academies or under private tutors. Written examinations were not employed, but applicants were admitted after personal interviews with the president or members of the faculty. Daniel Webster, at Dartmouth College, in 1797, presented a letter of recommendation from his tutor, the Reverend Samuel Wood, but also had to appear before several professors to be tested orally on his knowledge of Greek, Latin, English, and Arithmetic. Caleb Cushing took his entrance examinations at Harvard in 1813, at the age of thirteen; they were oral, lasting all day from six in the morning until six at night, with half an hour off for luncheon. He was quizzed in Greek, Latin, and Arithmetic, each one of twelve college officers taking a small section of applicants and passing it on when he had finished to one of his colleagues. At Amherst College, in 1822, the stated requirements for admission were Latin (Virgil, Cicero, and Sallust), Greek (Greek Testament and *Graeca Minora*), and what was delightfully called "Vulgar" Arithmetic. Just when written examinations were instituted at Harvard is not certain, but they were in vogue shortly after the mid-century. At Yale, entrance examinations were oral and informal until 1871.

By 1869—the *annus mirabilis* when Charles William Eliot became president of Harvard—public high schools were well established, and they increased in number from about forty in 1860 to nearly eight hundred in 1880. The amount of required Greek and Latin had not been reduced, but eight new possible entrance subjects had been added to the published lists—Geography, Algebra, Geometry, Physical Geography, English Grammar, English Composition, Ancient History, and United States History. It will be noted that neither the modern foreign languages nor the physical sciences were yet regarded as essential. These and English Literature were added before the close of the century. Harvard, far in advance of her competitors, began in 1874 to require a short test in English Composition. No examination in English was required for admission to Yale until 1893. At Amherst, in 1867, candidates were examined not only in Latin (Cicero, Virgil's *Aeneid* and the *Bucolics,* and

Sallust), Greek (three books of the *Anabasis* and two of the *Iliad*), Ancient Geography, Arithmetic, Algebra, and Geometry, but also in English Grammar, including Orthography and Orthoepy; and a sentence in the catalogue reads: "The examination in the common English branches will be insisted on with no less strictness than the Ancient Languages and the Mathematics." Largely because of President Eliot's leadership, American History, English Literature, and Science have since become staples of our school curricula.

Meanwhile each college was continuing its individual and oblivious way, altering the number and the quality of its admission requirements at will, until to an impartial outsider the situation approached the ridiculous. Wilson Farrand, headmaster of Newark Academy, expressed the views of his associates when he described the "unreasonable diversity" of college requirements. Nicholas Murray Butler, as a Columbia professor, declared that the colleges could agree "neither upon subjects to be offered for admission nor upon topics within these subjects," and added: "Each institution plays for its own hand, and consults first what it rightly or wrongly feels to be its peculiar interests; and then, if time and opportunity serve, it casts a sympathetic glance towards the interests of education in general."

Butler himself, matriculating at Columbia in 1878, took examinations in four books of Caesar's *Commentaries,* Sallust's *History,* Xenophon's *Anabasis,* Greek and Latin prose composition, and Ancient Geography— a subject in which he was conditioned because he was unable to recite in order, beginning with Greece and going eastward and northward all the way around to the

Euxine, the names both in Latin and in English, first of the capes and then of the rivers of Europe. It was probably the only test that he ever failed!

For the preparatory schools the uncertainty was both ludicrous and tragic. As Butler said, "If Cicero was prescribed, it meant in one place four orations and another six, and not always the same four or the same six." When some colleges demanded Greek Composition or Latin Composition, a school's classical department had to form special sections to meet the need. Each college, furthermore, held its entrance examinations to suit its convenience, with the result that the time schedule of a school like St. Paul's or Newton High School during the spring term was disrupted. One such group of examinations was set on the day of a school's most important baseball game, and the local protests were violent. Dr. Cecil F. P. Bancroft, principal of Phillips Academy, Andover, complained pathetically in 1885 that "out of over forty boys preparing for college next year we have more than twenty Senior classes." Andover liked to boast that it could prepare a candidate for any American college, but this became increasingly difficult when institutions continued to emphasize their unique and often absurd requirements. The written examinations themselves, often dictated hastily by professors with small knowledge of student psychology, were unscientific and varied in difficulty from year to year and from college to college. The only cure for this anomalous confusion was for the leading colleges to agree on some uniform standard. But not one of them was willing to yield its prerogatives. Each was a law unto itself. No central authority existed—or was desired.

One clear thinker, however, was dissatisfied with what he saw around him. William Allan Neilson always maintained that the inauguration of Charles W. Eliot as president of Harvard opened a new era in the history of American university education, and it could be truthfully added that his influence was salutary on education at all levels. The quality of Eliot's philosophy first was revealed in two revolutionary articles published in the *Atlantic Monthly* early in 1869, on "The New Education; Its Organization." Strongly affected by Herbert Spencer, Eliot rebelled against the rigid system of classical discipline then prevalent, advocating in its stead a program based chiefly upon the pure and applied sciences, the living European languages, and mathematics. Shortly afterwards, when he was barely thirty-five years old, he had been elected president of Harvard, and from then until he retired in 1909—and even after that—he engaged in an unceasing battle with entrenched conservatism wherever it appeared, especially on his own faculty. He was not always successful, but by the 1890's his reputation was international, and whatever views he chose to express were listened to with respect. Tall, erect, and dignified, with high standards and serious purposes, he seemed aloof and even frigid. His biographer, Henry James, described him as having "the calm look of a man whose patience and strength would be inexhaustible." His self-assurance and unconsciously imperious manner were impressive; it took a hardy opponent to stand up against him in debate. In his heart he was passionately devoted to what he conceived to be progress. In the introduction to a volume of his addresses rightly entitled *Educational Reform* (1898), he pointed out proudly that all the changes which he had later advocated had been distinctly though slightly outlined in his famous inaugural address at Harvard in 1869. "So slow is the progress of educational reform," he added, "so easy is it to discern educational improvements, so hard to get them carried into practice." In the agitation which culminated in the formation of the College Entrance Examination Board, his personality and character were at crucial moments decisive.

When Eliot, in 1877, suggested that something should be done to bring about co-operation among the colleges, his remarks had the effect of a feather falling upon a boulder. Even members of the Harvard faculty heard him with silent disapprobation. But he did start something, and some attempts were made during the next years to improve conditions. At a conference called in December, 1879, at Trinity College, in Hartford, Connecticut, a broad agreement was reached regarding desirable requirements in English; and similar meetings in 1881 and 1882 accomplished a partial clarification in the Classics and Mathematics. The formation of the New England Association of Colleges and Secondary Schools, in 1885, was significant, particularly in that it brought teachers on the two levels together. The purpose of this organization was indicated in its constitution, which stated, "Its object shall be the advancement of the cause of liberal education by the promotion of interests common to colleges and preparatory schools." Professor Corwin once pointed out that "it became and has remained the forum for the discussion of all current educational questions of importance."

It would appear that English teachers, elated that

their subject was at last receiving recognition, were especially eager to demonstrate their unanimity. A commission of New England Colleges in 1888 recommended the adoption of uniform requirements for intensive study. Soon boys and girls throughout the East were reading *Macbeth* and *The Merchant of Venice* (not yet under attack as a manifestation of racial hatred), Milton's *Minor Poems,* the *Sir Roger de Coverley Papers,* some of Macaulay's *Essays,* and even Burke's *Speech on Conciliation with the Colonies,* to say nothing of *The Ancient Mariner* and *Silas Marner,* the titles of which were inextricably confused in youthful minds. In 1895 a National Joint Conference on Uniform Entrance Requirements in English met in Boston for the first time and in 1898 had the audacity to recommend a full-time four-year preparatory course in that subject—a course which was shortly approved by almost a hundred colleges. Clearly the English teachers were blazing a trail for their associates in other fields to follow. What was happening in English was a significant sign of the times, a bright portent of better things to come.

The physical sciences, also coming into their own, moved more slowly, mainly because the science instruction in secondary schools was in such a deplorable state; but Harvard, under pressure from Eliot, initated an important movement by announcing in 1887 that it would require for admission a course of experiments in mechanics, sound, light, heat, and electricity. Soon the better schools equipped their own laboratories. Dr. Edwin C. Broome's *Historical and Critical Discussion of College Admission Requirements*—indispensable to any student of the subject—states that within a decade after Harvard's action nearly three times as many colleges insisted on Physics for admission to the Bachelor of Arts program as demanded a modern language.

Thus, by the 1890's the educational pot heated by President Eliot's burning words had really begun to boil. Furthermore aid was coming from other sources. The National Education Association, organized as far back as 1857, but for some years impotent, had been revived in 1884 and under vigorous young leadership was preparing to lend a hand. At its meeting in Toronto in 1891 a group of high school principals assailed bitterly the policies governing college admission. Even when colleges had taken most of their students from private preparatory schools specializing in the Greek and Roman classics, the problem was sometimes difficult; but with the spread and improvement of the public high school, a different type of training was spreading over the country. One principal at Toronto asked, "How can I treat my students who are looking forward to entering different colleges at which examinations for admission are held at different times, with different requirements and sharply differing definitions of one and the same nominal requirement?" No one seems to have been able to answer him at the moment. Fortunately, however, Professor Nicholas Murray Butler—the "Nicholas Miraculous" of a later generation—was there to listen and to plan what could be done.

Born on April 2, 1862, in New Jersey, Butler was graduated from Columbia in the Class of 1882, and after graduate study in Europe he became, in 1885, assistant in Philosophy at his alma mater, where he remained in various capacities until his retirement as president in

1945. A paragon of omniscience and versatility, Butler was rather overwhelming in his vitality, touching many phases—social, political, and intellectual—of the life around him. During the 1890's he was obviously the "white-headed boy" of the American collegiate world; he himself recorded that between 1886 and 1899 he was offered the presidency of eight state universities, including California and Wisconsin, and was also begged by Governor Leland Stanford to be the first president of Stanford University. Butler, however, thought he saw a wider opportunity before him at Columbia, and it turned out that he was right. When President Low was persuaded in the autumn of 1901 to run for mayor of New York City, everybody on Morningside Heights looked to the indefatigable, ubiquitous, and aggressive professor of Psychology and Education as the inevitable next president of Columbia.

The *Educational Review,* which Butler started in January, 1891, served as an acceptable medium for presenting ideas in which the young editor was interested—among them a college admissions board. Writing on March 6, 1925, to Professor Thomas S. Fiske, Butler said, "I certainly do regard the College Entrance Examination Board as one of my educational children, since it was my own conception and I had to do all the hard work in getting it authorized and organized." At the meeting in Toronto already mentioned, he seems to have taken charge of the discussion and quickly found himself named chairman of a committee of representatives from colleges and secondary schools to consider the plight of the high school principals. This committee, at the next meeting of the National Education Association, in 1892, at Saratoga, introduced a motion calling for the appointment of a committee of ten, to be charged with the investigation of the entire subject of the relations between schools and colleges. With characteristic boldness, Butler induced President Eliot to serve as chairman of the committee; and the latter conscientiously devoted a large amount of his time and strength to preparing what turned out to be a document of the highest significance. An editorial in the *Educational Review* asserted that Eliot was from the beginning the dominant figure in the deliberations of the committee and took the heaviest share of the burden on himself.

The ensuing *Report* was not, however, a "one-man job," for Eliot had some thoughtful and influential associates. William T. Harris, United States Commissioner of Education from 1889 to 1906, described by Butler with some exaggeration as "the one great philosophical mind which has appeared on this side of the Atlantic," was a member, as was also the modest, talented, and liberal James B. Angell, president of the University of Michigan from 1871 to 1909. These were educators of national, even international prominence. Other college presidents, selected partly for geographical considerations, were James M. Taylor, of Vassar, Richard H. Jones, of Missouri, and James H. Baker, of Colorado. The secondary representatives were John Tetlow, of the Boston Girls' Latin School, Oscar D. Robinson, of Albany Academy, and Headmaster James C. Mackenzie, of Lawrenceville School. Rounding out the impressive list was the scholarly and eloquent Henry C. King, at that time professor of Philosophy at Oberlin and later for a quarter of a century president of that col-

lege. It was this Committee of Ten which finally outlined what has been called "the first comprehensive
program of secondary education" and did the spadework
necessary before the College Entrance Examination
Board could be formed.

The directors of the National Education Association
broke one of their precedents by voting the committee
an appropriation of $2,100 for expenses. Although But-
ler was not officially a member, he entertained the committee for their first meeting at his house in Stuyvesant
Square and arranged for their subsequent sessions in
the trustees' room of old Columbia College. Their major task was to achieve a semblance of uniformity by
outlining courses of study and fixing minimum standards for secondary schools. Nine subcommittees were
appointed to examine prevailing practices and report
their findings. Eventually the committee laid down the
fundamental principle that every school should provide
for continuous instruction in the four main fields of
knowledge, which were classified as Language (including English), Mathematics, History, and Science. This
program, so radically different from the narrow curriculum of the eighteenth century, undoubtedly reflected
the liberal philosophy of President Eliot. Professor Corwin has said of the report: "It became a Declaration of
Rights in behalf of the high school, of non-classical
studies, and of the pupil who was not preparing for college."

One gratifying aspect of the committee's procedure
was the willingness of the collegiate members to listen
to the three secondary school representatives—Tetlow,
Robinson, and Mackenzie. President Eliot, in an ad-

dress delivered on July 11, 1894, before the American Institute of Instruction, commented on this fact as follows:

On the whole the greatest promise of usefulness which I see in the Report of the Committee of Ten lies in its obvious tendency to promote cooperation among school and college teachers, and all other persons intelligently interested in education, for the advancement of well-marked and comprehensive educational reforms.

In this large-scale research project the public schools were for the first time assigned their proper place in the foreground of the American educational picture, and their objectives were given careful consideration. The necessity for complete democracy and freedom of expression was early recognized by the committee, and this perhaps accounts for the later sensitivity of the College Entrance Examination Board to well-intentioned, intelligent criticism. Indeed, in several ways the Committee of Ten developed a tone and spirit which were afterwards inherited by the board.

The Committee of Ten, while well aware of the insistent problem of college admissions and of the restiveness of the schools, took no formal action on the matter, confining itself to what it conceived to be the broader phases of education. In November, 1894, however, President Eliot, reporting to the New England Association, made the suggestion that the colleges organize a board of examiners to conduct all over the country admissions examinations, the certified results of which should be good at all the New England colleges and good anywhere else where the certificates of the board would be accepted.

Dr. Eliot said later, "I hardly think that the proposition was regarded by the Association of Colleges as one seriously to be taken up. At any rate it was not taken up." The campaign of education had not yet shown results.

Meanwhile other people were doing some thinking, some listening, and a good deal of talking. The Headmasters' Association, founded in 1893, brought together an influential body of private and public school men, headed by Dr. Bancroft, of Andover, their first president. At all their early meetings it was evident that the members, although deeply concerned over the matter of uniform college admission requirements, were at a loss how most effectively to make themselves felt. At their fourth gathering, in 1895, at Philadelphia, Dr. Julius Sachs presented the topic, "Suggestions for Improved Methods of Conducting College Entrance Examinations," and the open discussion which followed gave several complainants a chance to unburden their souls. The secretary of the Association reported in his minutes that "there seemed to be held out the reasonable prospect of an early adjustment of the difficulties which now annoy the secondary schools by reason of the varying requirements for admission to colleges." This meeting, and others which came after, were by no means unimportant steps in the gradual crystallization of public opinion—an essential part of the democratic process. There were still, of course, those skeptics and pessimists who were disposed to mutter, using the language of Calvin Coolidge, "Won't anything come of it!"

The most comprehensive and pungent indictment of the general disorder in education was uttered by Wilson Farrand, of Newark Academy, in his inaugural address as president of the Schoolmasters' Association of New York and vicinity, delivered on October 12, 1895. Speaking on the topic "The Reform of College Entrance Requirements," he ridiculed the inconsistencies in the entrance requirements of Harvard, Yale, Princeton, and Columbia. From the evidence as he presented it I have excerpted some pertinent sentences:

The more closely we examine the details, the more marked are the differences. For instance, Princeton and Columbia call for six books of the *Aeneid;* Yale requires, in addition, the *Eclogues.* These do not count for maximum standing at Princeton unless combined with the *Georgics.* The elementary Algebra requirement at Harvard is less than is exacted of students at Princeton and Yale; her advanced requirement is greater. . . .

When we come to the Scientific Schools, the discrepancies are even greater. Princeton requires Latin of candidates for one course, but not for the others. Yale demands it of all, Columbia of none. Princeton names five books of Caesar and four orations of Cicero; Yale names four books of Caesar and three books of Virgil. . . . Yale calls for Botany, Columbia for Physics and Chemistry, Princeton for no science. Princeton and Columbia demand both German and French, while Yale is satisfied with either. On the other hand, while Princeton and Columbia demand only American History, Yale calls also for that of England. . . .

For our Princeton boys we must include a review of Arithmetic and carry Algebra farther than is required by Harvard or Columbia; for Yale we must read the Bucolics and study Logarithms and their application to geometrical problems; for Harvard we must supply a thorough course in Physics. . . . Look again, for a moment, at the requirements in science. Harvard puts on a stiff requirement in Physics, Columbia lighter ones in Physics and Chemistry, Yale calls for Botany, Cornell for Physiology.

Farrand then paid his respects to "the personal idiosyncrasies of the individual examiner."

I have been told by a college professor, when I objected to a certain question, that he had put it there simply to call the attention of preparatory schools to that point. We all of us have seen papers that were apparently constructed on the same basis. . . . The individual element is also clearly shown by the entire absence of any uniform standard of thoroughness or difficulty. A subject will be most rigorously treated at one college, and most indulgently at another. In the same college the examination in one subject will most justly be regarded as a "terror" and that in another as a "perfect snap." . . . I am speaking to an audience of teachers, and every teacher has in his possession a choice assortment of entrance examination curiosities.

Next Farrand mentioned the "grave distrust" which existed as to the accuracy and justice with which the entrance examination papers were judged and cited several cases of "inexcusable blunders and errors of judgment." He ended the argument for the prosecution by stating that with few exceptions the examinations attempted too much, by trying in the space of two or three hours to test the extent and thoroughness of work that had filled from two to five years. He closed with an axiom which will bear frequent repetition: "The ideal entrance examination will attempt to discover not so much what the candidate has done as what he can do."

Farrand did not at this time actually suggest a college

entrance examination board. As partial remedies for the evils enumerated he proposed (1) that a certificate be submitted from the candidate's principal instructor; (2) that examinations be made general rather than specific; (3) that the decision regarding admission be reached by the college on the basis of both the certificate and the examinations; (4) that the college provide for administering examinations accurately, fairly, and wisely; and (5) that the requirements of the various colleges be made uniform. To attain these ends, he advocated first agitation and then legislation—either a central commission or committee, not unlike the Committee of Ten, whose sole duty should be to investigate the whole subject of entrance requirements and to propose a scheme for their unification, or a separate committee for each subject, made up of experts representing the various parts of the country and the different classes of higher and secondary institutions. He concluded:

It is the first step that counts. A long step forward has been taken in the department of English, and there is no valid reason why in the coming year a similar step should not be taken in some other department. The essential thing to secure this action is a distinct and united demand on the part of schoolmasters. Agitation will compel legislation, and through agitation and legislation we shall attain the desired end.

Farrand's carefully prepared address was one out of many indications that, as Professor Robert N. Corwin said, "school men were losing patience with the alleged prescience and assumed authority of the college professor in matters pertaining to admission to college." It elicited many comments, some of them amusing. Profes sor Daniels, of the Princeton Department of Economics wrote rather cynically:

The securing of uniform entrance requirements is, venture to think, a task of perhaps greater difficulty than you imagine. There is first the difficulty of one college' making overtures to another. It is a fact, though a disagree able one, that such overtures are regarded by Colleg Faculties with aversion. The recipient college is not unap to fear the *Danaos et dona ferentes,* and to put the matte off with a few courteous words familiar to college diplo macy, but which really mean that they fear they may be "buncoed" in the proposed deal.

Further than this as regards the Science requirement I do not see how Harvard can consent to abolish that re quirement in Physics, so long as her elective system doe not exact a course in that subject from all her under graduates.

Lastly, even with approximate uniformity secured in nominal requirements, "differences of administration" would not infrequently nullify the effect thereof. College are not above rate-cutting any more than railroads.

William C. Collar, the distinguished headmaster of the Roxbury Latin School, wished that "a copy could be put into the hands of every college professor in the country," and then went on:

What you say about the widespread distrust of the care and accuracy with which examinations are conducted is very true. I have from Harvard College an official statement of the results of the preliminary and final examinations of my boys last June. In this statement a boy in my second class, who did not go within four miles of the college, is credited with passing in most of the elementary subjects and in several advanced subjects, some of which he had never studied. I think it will be hard to match that!

The movement thus sponsored by so many well-informed teachers was by this time gaining real headway. The National Education Association, at its meeting in 1895 at Denver, formed a Committee on College Entrance Requirements, authorized to study current procedures and consider methods of making them more nearly uniform. This so-called Committee of Twelve collected and tabulated the published requirements of sixty-seven leading colleges, east, west, north, and south, and called attention to their astounding diversity. The conclusions of this committee were submitted in 1899, after four years of intermittent research and conference, in fourteen brief resolutions, which could never have been regarded as acceptable if the issues had not been threshed out at many a fireside and in the give-and-take of debate.

The Committee of Twelve agreed that it was inadvisable for all American colleges to lay down the same entrance requirements, or for all schools to provide the same courses of study. What it hoped was that the colleges would be persuaded to state their entrance requirements in terms of national units, or norms, and that the schools in their turn would construct their curriculums from the units furnished by these specifications. On its face, as we read it today, this *Report* seems irrefutable —so rational, and so constructive, that it is almost trite. The truth is that while it was being prepared educational missionaries had effected many a conversion. Dr. Broome made a natural observation when he wrote that the *Report* offered "a feasible means of securing elasticity, and at the same time uniformity, in secondary schools." In all its argument it never forgot the desirability of a close articulation between schools and colleges— a fact which commended it at once to members of the Headmasters' Association. The next, and final, step was to turn this delightful theory into practice. This could be done only by sympathetic co-operation of the kind so eloquently advocated by President Eliot.

In the midst of all this argument "about it and about," Butler had been working in his usual practical fashion. At a meeting of the Columbia faculty on December 22, 1893, he had introduced a resolution calling upon the president to enter into correspondence with colleges and scientific schools in the East with a view to establishing a College Admission Examination Board which would hold tests at one and the same time in conveniently accessible centers, such examinations to replace as soon as practicable those offered at the various separate institutions. As Butler anticipated, the motion was laid on the table, for it was too unexpected, probably too radical, to be voted upon without deliberation. Indeed, if a show of hands had been called for on the spot, it would have been overwhelmingly defeated. But with the skill of a consummate politician Butler pursued his campaign of educating the proper people. He won over Columbia's president, Seth Low, rather easily, together with some of his own colleagues. Although he had numerous other schemes in his fertile mind, he never forgot this particular project and was content to bide his time. On February 28, 1896, without any fuss or modification, his resolution passed the faculty unanimously.

In that same month and under President Low's sponsorship an interesting and profitable Conference on Uniform Entrance Requirements was held at Columbia, participated in by Columbia, Cornell, Harvard, Pennsylvania, Princeton, and Yale—what newspaper men like to call the Big Six—together with some carefully selected men from the secondary schools, public and private. Although this meeting broke up without formulating any definite plan, further strides towards unity had been taken. It is true that the smaller colleges were chary of any innovation emanating from Harvard and Columbia; and it was a trifle disconcerting that President Patton, of Princeton, had not been enthusiastic over the proposals. But the possibility of some agreement seemed less remote than when Butler had first undertaken his crusade.

The weary years of complaint and apparently futile discussion reached a climax at the meeting on December 2, 1899, in Trenton, New Jersey, of the Association of Colleges and Secondary Schools of the Middle States and Maryland. Butler had decided in advance that the hour had arrived for the presentation of a formal resolution calling in specific terms for the establishment of a College Admissions Board. President Eliot, learning of Butler's intention and wishing to support him, left Cambridge and came all the way to Trenton by the night train, although he was not, of course, a member of the Middle States Association. Thus, the two leaders were there together—Eliot the older by some twenty-eight years, but equally eager to win the victory. Eliot was reserved and introverted; Butler was an expansive extrovert. Eliot was calm and deliberate; Butler was impulsive. Together they symbolized the best in American higher education.

Three topics had been assigned for consideration at this meeting; the second was "Uniform College Admission Requirements, with a Joint Board of Examiners." At the appropriate moment Butler rose, offered his resolutions, and spoke briefly in their favor. He asserted that most of the difficulties which had attended, and did still attend, the relations between secondary schools and colleges grew out of "our educational atomism," or local self-sufficiency. After reviewing the causes of the existing confusion, he continued:

To remove these crying and admitted evils, there is need, not alone of uniform requirements for college admission, but of a uniform administration of these requirements. To establish uniform requirements without uniform administration would leave the problem unsolved.

Butler stoutly predicted that if this were done "within five years a new and now almost unknown atmosphere of satisfaction and comfort would surround the work of college preparation." He felt that "all this unrest is to usher in an era of educational cooperation which will increase the effectiveness of our existing machinery manifold."

Butler was followed, according to arrangement, by Principal Christopher Gregory, of Long Branch, New Jersey, representing the public schools, who in measured language substantiated all that his predecessor had said. Then the fireworks began. President Patton, of Princeton, speaking for the Old Guard, rose and plausibly defended the current practice. Next, President Ethelbert D. Warfield, of Lafayette College, a young man, only slightly older than Butler, secured the floor and rather solemnly protested that such a board would invade the rights of the colleges and restrict their privilege of selecting their own students.

Lafayette College does not intend [he declared pompously] to be told by any Board whom to admit and whom not to admit. If we wish to admit the son of a benefactor, or of a Trustee, or of a member of the Faculty, and such action will benefit the institution, we are not going to be· prevented from taking it.

As he listened, Eliot realized that unforeseen circumstances had delivered his opponent into his hands. It was precisely the situation which he relished most, and he improved it. Rising and standing as usual so stiff that he seemed almost to be bending slightly backwards, with his heels close together and his hands gripped tightly in front of him, he began slowly, without any display of emotion, to speak in general terms of the advantages of Butler's plan. Then with a faint smile on his austere countenance, he turned to look at Warfield and said:

The President of Lafayette College has misunderstood Mr. Butler's proposal. The College Entrance Examination Board, if constituted, is not to admit students to any college, but so to define the subjects of admission that they will be uniform, to conduct examinations in these subjects at uniform times throughout the world, and to issue to those who take the examinations certificates of performance,—good, bad, or indifferent. And, President Warfield, it will be perfectly practicable under this plan for Lafayette College to say, if it chooses, that it will admit only such students as cannot pass these examinations. No one proposes to deprive Lafayette College of that privilege.

As these telling words fell from Eliot's lips, the assemblage broke into unrestrained laughter and then into loud applause. Warfield and the opposition were completely silenced. Other speakers, including President Low and four preparatory school principals, argued in support of Butler, but their aid was not needed. The temper of the meeting was easily felt, and when the vote was taken the association declared itself unanimously for the establishment of the new board. Butler wrote later, "This might never have happened if President Eliot had not come down from Cambridge to support the proposal and make that kind of speech."

It is noteworthy that Butler's plan as outlined at the Trenton meeting envisioned with clarity and detail the organization of the College Entrance Examination Board as it shortly was set up. He had bestowed plenty of thought on the difficulties which had to be surmounted. He had prepared himself to answer all possible criticism, fair or unfair, and was ready to correct discernible weaknesses. It was typical of him that, like Eliot, he could see the panorama as a whole and was willing to sacrifice, if necessary, his own college in order to secure a demonstrable gain for all American education. His breadth of view, his comprehension of educational problems on various levels, from kindergarten to university, his wide acquaintance with his professional colleagues—all these kept him from major blunders.

Historically, then, the College Entrance Examination Board was the direct consequence of a gradual clarification of thought which took place during the last quarter of the nineteenth century in an effort to make education a sound process of evolution. The original idea sprang from the fertile mind of Charles William Eliot; the transference into action came largely from the vital spirit of Nicholas Murray Butler. There is glory enough for both of them—and for the many others who, in lesser ways, furnished comfort and support.

CHAPTER II

EARLY

ORGANIZATION

IT MUST NOT be forgotten that the College Entrance Examination Board was organized, under Professor Butler's resolutions, as the instrument of the Association of Colleges and Secondary Schools of the Middle States and Maryland. An editorial in the *Educational Review* for January, 1900, said:

It has fallen to the lot of this Association to follow up the long-drawn-out discussions of college entrance examinations with substantive action. . . . In time the relations between secondary school and college will become normal and educational instead of abnormal and pedagogical.

The original call, dated December 14, 1899, less than two weeks after the memorable meeting at Trenton, was signed by the heads of four Middle States colleges— Charles C. Harrison, provost of the University of Pennsylvania; Seth Low, president of Columbia University; A. V. V. Raymond, president of Union University; and Jacob G. Schurman, president of Cornell University. These were all gentlemen well known to the general public; in fact, it would have been impossible to find a better sponsorship in that area. Four women's colleges —Barnard, Vassar, Bryn Mawr, and the Woman's College of Baltimore—immediately responded, as did Columbia, Colgate, Pennsylvania, New York University, Union, Rutgers, Princeton, and Cornell. The Trenton resolutions had authorized the Executive Committee to designate representatives of secondary schools, and three were accordingly named—Wilson Farrand, Julius Sachs, and Edward Jasper Goodwin.

Wilson Farrand was for so many years actively identified with the Board that it was possible for him in 1925 to recollect vividly what he called "significant events,—natal, pre-natal, infantile, and adolescent,—in the life of the organization." Born in 1862, he was almost precisely the same age as Nicholas Murray Butler, and he lived to be eighty. At the time of his death, in 1942, he was serving as the board's Chief Custodian and attending all its meetings with regularity. It was at his invitation that President Eliot came from Cambridge to speak in 1896 before the Schoolmasters' Association of New York and vicinity and that President Low attended from Columbia and endorsed Eliot's radical proposals. One of a family of distinguished brothers, Farrand was graduated from Princeton in 1886 and became first a teacher at Newark Academy and then successively associate headmaster and headmaster, retiring in 1935 with an *emeritus* status. For many years he was a trustee of Princeton and clerk of the Board. He was a thin wisp of a man, meticulous in his dress and manner, with an intellectual profile and piercing eyes. He had a crisp wit, accentuated by an apologetic little cough preceding a clever phrase. Because of his gift for lucidity and condensation, he was selected for many years by the Headmasters' Association to sum up its proceedings at their final dinner. Urbane, politely deferential, and yet

firm when firmness was necessary, he early won the re
spect of the collegiate members of the Board, who knew
that they could rely on his sagacity and imagination.

Julius Sachs, in 1899, was considerably older than
Farrand, and in some respects had had a more varied
experience. He had served on several committees of na
tional importance and had fought valiantly through
all the formative stages for the new Board. Trained after
graduating from Columbia in foreign universities, he
was temperamentally a scholar, but a scholar with a
practical conception of the relationship of classroom
education to actual life. From the beginning he insisted
that the Board should not be satisfied merely with the
machinery for measuring achievement, but should also
"promote definite improvement in the spirit of our sec
ondary schools," even going so far as to advocate a study
and an interpretation of the records of certain schools
and teachers through a succession of years. In 1925, at
the twenty-fifth anniversary of the Board, after he had
retired as professor of Education at Teachers College,
he stressed the point that the effectiveness of the Board
had been due to the co-operation of the members in their
attempt to produce what he called "unified expert
thought." Farrand once spoke eulogistically of Sachs'
"encyclopedic scholarship, sound judgment, unfailing
common sense, and unswerving persistence." Bearded
and erudite, thoroughly Teutonic in his experience and
reactions, he brought something a little out of the ordi
nary into committee meetings. No one had a broader
conception than he of the possibilities for good inherent
in such an organization as the Board; and in those early

days he worked through many channels in a passionate desire to accomplish his aims.

The third of the secondary school triumvirate was Edward Joseph Goodwin, a Bates College graduate who from 1887 to 1897 was principal of the excellent high school in Newton, Massachusetts, and then transferred to New York as head of the Morris High School. He and Sachs were charter members of the Headmasters' Association, and Farrand was elected to that organization as soon as his appointment as headmaster made him eligible. Although the three were quite different in temperament, they were united in their loyalty to the Board and could present acceptably the secondary school opinions and hopes. Many of the older high-ranking schools, like Roxbury Latin, Boston Latin, Andover, Exeter, and St. Paul's, were located in New England and therefore could not be identified with a Middle States project.

Although it had taken many years to secure the legal sanction, the advocates of the new Board, once the vote had been passed, moved with what was, for educators, uncommon celerity. The group of seventeen, with Butler still the motivating spirit, met in the new library of Columbia, on Morningside Heights, where that university had moved two years earlier. President Low, the official host, was complimented by being elected chairman, and Farrand was chosen secretary. It was promptly agreed that the proposed organization should be christened "The College Entrance Examination Board." Because it proved to be a cumbersome title, there has been a tendency to abbreviate it to "College Entrance

Board" or even, more simply, "College Board," by which name it is familiarly known today. A subcommittee consisting of Butler, as chairman, Professor West, of Princeton, Dean White, of Cornell, Mr. Farrand, and Mr. Goodwin was appointed to draft a constitution and rules. With due caution the group made it clear that no member was necessarily committed to the plan, but that "every college shall be free to take part or not to take part in the administration of the Board so established, and to accept or not to accept the results of examinations as certified by such Board." The promoters were moving prudently, anxious to avoid the insinuation of dictatorship and wishing not to antagonize those who had been either critical or indifferent to their designs.

The subcommittee was urged to study systems of examinations in this and other countries, and at Butler's instigation it was particularly voted that the recent "Report of the Committee of Twelve" of the National Education Association, which had appeared in the *Proceedings* of the National Education Association for 1899, should be used as a guide to their deliberations. Something has already been said in Chapter I of the quality of this report, with its fourteen resolutions. The very first resolution accepted the principle of election as valid in secondary schools. Its sixth, however, expressed the conviction that there should be a certain number of "constants" in all secondary schools and in all requirements for admission to college, including four units in Foreign Language (no language accepted in fewer than two units), two units in Mathematics, two in English, one in History, and one in Science. A unit was broadly defined as "at least one year of four periods a week in a well-equipped secondary school under competent instruction." All subjects were thus placed on parity so far as their relative value in admission requirements was concerned, and there was no unfair discrimination in favor of any field of study, classical or mathematical. The report endeavored to "set forth a series of interchangeable units of substantially the same value" that would constitute a form of educational currency, or negotiable notes, acceptable in any school throughout the country maintaining courses approximately equivalent in content and standards to those outlined by the Committee of Twelve.

The Committee of Twelve recommended that teachers in secondary schools should have collegiate degrees and approved of encouraging gifted students to complete the preparatory course in less time than was required for average pupils. It also suggested that the school day should be lengthened to permit a larger amount of study in school under supervision. But these matters have no real relevance to this narrative. Dr. Broome, whose study of their report is painstaking and intelligent, is right in saying:

The distinct contribution of the report of the committee is the suggestions that the units should be of a definite and national value, that they form the material from which all secondary school programs may be composed, and that they be accepted at par value in all schools and colleges.

It has already been pointed out that this report, perhaps because it was more reconcilable than had been supposed with current educational ideas and practices, met with almost universal approval. Its adoption as a guide by the College Entrance Examination Board offered positive assurance that the Board would proceed with discretion. Butler and his associates were aware that their efforts must at first be concentrated on winning the support of teachers for the new Board and its philosophy. The certificate, or diploma, system of admission to college was in the 1890's very popular, especially in the state colleges of the Middle West. The University of Michigan had established an accrediting system as early as 1870, and it was estimated in 1897 that at least 42 state colleges and about 150 other institutions on the higher level employed some form of certificating plan. It certainly had stanch advocates among those who felt that, with its procedure of inspection, visitation, and regular correspondence, it brought the schools and colleges more intimately together. Even President Eliot once argued that when efficiently operated it was almost ideal. Its best features have, of course, been preserved by some of our most exacting colleges, as supplementary to the Board's examinations.

Many who believed theoretically in examinations had confidence only in those which they set themselves. The Board of Regents in the State of New York had for some years conducted examinations in a variety of subjects at the academies and high schools of the state and had issued to those who passed them certificates good for their face value in New York colleges and indeed in other areas. I can well recall being admitted to Amherst College in 1901 solely on the basis of "Regents' credits." But the system had quite justly been subjected to severe criticism. In an article in the *Arena* for June, 1890, on

"The Gap between Common Schools and Colleges," President Eliot had declared, without mincing words, that the examination papers of the Board of Regents did not proceed "from a body of men of recognized authority in teaching"; that the examinations were conducted without supervision by any agent of the Regents; and that the quality of the examiners was very far from being respected. As a student in a New York State rural high school during that period, I can testify that the examinations were uneven in value, often absurdly easy, and sometimes not uniformly, or even honestly, administered. Persons familiar with the Regents's system in operation had good reason for being dubious about any similar plan on a larger scale, no matter how well guaranteed.

It was obvious, then, that the new Board must make immediately a scientific study of examinations—a function which was shortly to become one of its most significant and profitable undertakings. President Eliot, in the *Arena* article just mentioned, spoke favorably of the methods employed at Harvard in preparing papers for its admission examinations. The school men, however, were not always so favorably impressed, and even Eliot admitted that mistakes in judgment had been occasionally perpetrated. The traditional type of examination, drafted frequently in haste and with little knowledge of the basic principles of educational psychology, was vulnerable to attack by experienced secondary school teachers. It should be axiomatic that unless examinations are a reasonably accurate measure of ability and training, they are worse than useless. Dr. Butler and his committee perceived that a considerable amount of experimentation must be entered upon before satisfactory results could be expected. It is rather remarkable, under the circumstances, that the Board gained prestige so quickly.

The enlightening report of the Committee of Twelve had already indicated the conditions under which uniformity in admission requirements was possible. It was now the business of the College Entrance Examination Board to demonstrate that it could be achieved. Composed as it was of both college and school representatives, it brought the two groups together for practical ends and mutual profit. It was altogether good that college administrators and secondary school teachers should meet, interchanging opinions and subordinating prejudices. As a medium for removing misunderstandings and promoting friendships among members of the teaching profession, the College Entrance Examination Board has been unsurpassed in this country.

On May 12, 1900, a group of seventeen men and women, most of them already publicly identified with the Board project, met to receive the Report of Butler's subcommittee. After some discussion and the acceptance of some unimportant verbal amendments, this was formally adopted as a *Plan of Organization and Permanent Constitution.* The chairman, President Low, was then authorized to transmit copies of this Plan of Organization to the several colleges invited to participate, with the request that each notify him as soon as practicable, and if possible before July 1, 1900, whether it would accept it and appoint a representative to the new College Entrance Examination Board, and also whether it would accept for admission the certificates issued as a result of the Board examinations. The subcommittee, which had done its job thoroughly, next submitted other items—a list of nine subjects in which it was proposed to hold examinations; definitions of the requirements in each subject; and a set of forms of examination records. Butler and Farrand, who throughout these proceedings saw one another frequently and worked amicably together, were named a committee to edit and distribute copies of the *Plan of Organization* where they would do the most good.

The *Plan of Organization and Constitution,* printed as "Document No. 2" in the Board's publications, lasted for many years without revision. After outlining the qualifications for membership and the various offices to be filled, it stipulated that in each subject the Board should designate a college teacher to act as Chief Examiner and one additional college teacher and one secondary school teacher to serve as Associate Examiners. It also provided for a staff of Readers "to inspect and give a rating to the answer books, or other tests, offered at the examinations." Answer books were to be graded on a scale of 100, and no answer book was to be irrevocably marked below 60 until it had been passed upon by two Readers. The fee for each candidate was set at $5. Other technical details are relatively unimportant here. It is sufficient to say that the subcommittee had foreseen nearly every complicating question.

On November 17, 1900, the organization of the College Entrance Examination Board was formally announced, with the following twelve institutional and charter members: Barnard College, Bryn Mawr College, Columbia University, Cornell University, Johns Hopkins University, New York University, Rutgers College,

Swarthmore College, Union College, University of Pennsylvania, Vassar College, and the Woman's College of Baltimore. Colgate and Princeton, which had been in the original group, were not yet ready officially to join. Thus the Board became a reality without the active support of Harvard, Yale, or Princeton. Yale and Princeton, however, soon advised the Secretary of their willingness to accept the Board's examinations as satisfactory substitutes for their own. Despite President Eliot's large share in the preliminary negotiations, Harvard did not associate itself with the Board until 1904.

The *Plan of Organization* authorized the Association of Colleges and Secondary Schools of the Middle States and Maryland to choose annually five representatives of the secondary schools as members of the Board. The men thus selected were Wilson Farrand and Julius Sachs, whose activities have already been mentioned; Walter B. Gunnison, principal of Erasmus Hall High School, Brooklyn, since 1885; John Meigs, founder and headmaster of the Hill School, Pottstown, Pennsylvania, since 1876; and Joseph S. Walton, of Philadelphia.

Throughout this period of organization, Professor Butler was tireless, resourceful, and optimistic. At one of the many meetings of the subcommittee Wilson Farrand asked how, when everybody knew how many mistakes in recording were made by college registrars concerning only two or three hundred candidates, it would be possible to ensure reasonable accuracy with ten times that number involved. Butler replied:

A bank or trust company, by a carefully devised system of checks and balances, is able to carry thousands of accounts without the variation of a cent; and it must be possible to work out a system of checks which will ensure equal accuracy in the record of any number of examinations.

Furthermore Butler, like a good general, never forgot that the Board must forestall attack. In one of its first published documents he drafted a statement of the manifest advantages of the Board examinations, listing them as follows:

(1) That they are uniform in subject matter.
(2) That they are uniformly administered.
(3) That they are held at many points, to meet the convenience of students, at one and the same time.
(4) That they represent a cooperative effort on the part of a group of colleges, no one of which thereby surrenders its individuality.
(5) That by reason of their uniformity they will aid greatly the work of the secondary schools.
(6) That they will tend to effect a marked saving of time, money, and effort in administering college admission requirements.

Having learned that any complicated piece of administrative machinery requires in its human relations not only motive power but lubrication, Butler saw to it that good work was fittingly recognized. He also endeavored to enlist the aid of people who were captious or potentially hostile. Aware of the jealousies lying dormant in men accustomed to command, he avoided being too conspicuous or autocratic. More than once by tactful words he averted trouble.

A few of the secondary schools, especially those which were long established and sure of themselves, were coy and even reluctant to join in the new venture. But the projectors were not overly disturbed by the lack of immediate or unanimous support. It took months for even the Constitution of the United States to win the necessary popular approval. The officers of the Board had to move charily at first to keep from treading on self-satisfied and haughty toes. Perhaps for this reason the early reports of the Board spent time in reiterating that it was not, and from the nature of things could not be, bureaucratic or greedy or dangerously assertive.

Crucial in the policy of the Board as it prepared for its first test was the choice of Examiners. The colleges had too frequently assigned the making of examinations to superannuated professors or cub instructors, with consequences which the secondary schools never wearied of emphasizing. I well remember how President Butler, in one of his after-dinner monologues at The Breakers, Palm Beach, recounted some of his difficulties.

It was necessary [he said] to select teachers whom everybody in their field knew and respected. But we couldn't just pick them for window dressing. They would have to work, and the whole Board would be judged by what they did. They were to prepare examinations for an extraordinarily critical body of secondary school teachers, sensitive and proud, teachers who knew how and where the Regents' examinations had failed. If the tests were too easy, teachers would laugh; if they were too hard, they would complain. Furthermore we had only the Middle States to choose from, and that left out a good many fine men from New England and from some of the best colleges. Sometimes I think it was the hardest job I ever did.

The examination subjects as finally agreed upon were nine in number—Chemistry, English, French, German, Greek, History, Latin, Mathematics, and Physics—

Botany and Zoology having been dropped for good and sufficient reasons. The definition of the requirement in each was taken from the recommendations of national committees: for example, the requirements in Latin were based on the recommendations of the American Philological Association; those in French met the demands of the Committee of Twelve of the Modern Language Association; and the requirement in History followed closely the outline submitted by the Committee of Seven of the American Historical Association. This wise policy ensured from the beginning the maintenance of the highest existing standards.

The important matter, however, was to get the right Examiners, both men and women—for three women were included in the list. No critics could say much that was derogatory about such leaders as Professor Francis H. Stoddard, of New York University, in English, Professor Charles E. Bennett, of Cornell, in Latin, and Professor A. Guyot Cameron, of Princeton, in French; the other Chief Examiners were almost equally distinguished. The secondary school representatives, one in each subject, were also well known, including Principal Henry P. Warren, of Albany Academy, in History, Thomas B. Bronson, of the Lawrenceville School, in German, Principal Frank D. Boynton, of the Ithaca High School, in Physics, and Miss Helen J. Robins, of Miss Baldwin's School, in English. These and others who are omitted only because of lack of space were scholars not likely to associate themselves with any fly-by-night project. They were among the best that the East had to offer.

The Chief Examiners, on whom so much depended,

were formally appointed on November 17, 1900—the
date which is accepted for the actual birth of the College
Entrance Examination Board. The Associate Examiners were not named until January 12, 1901. The nine
groups of three met almost at once to establish criteria
and procedures. On March 23 the so-called Committee
of Revision, consisting of the nine Chief Examiners,
together with the five representatives of secondary
schools on the Board, assembled in New York and spent
hours going over the questions in each subject, making
sure that they were of approximately the same difficulty
and were genuine tests of proficiency and sound teaching. Wilson Farrand said later that this Committee of
Revision kept the Board from perpetrating some very
serious blunders.

The papers in their revised form were ready for printing on April 1, and the examinations themselves were
held during the week beginning June 17, 1901, at 67
centers in the United States and 2 in Europe. They
were attended by 973 candidates, of whom 758 were
seeking admission to either Columbia College or Barnard College. It was obvious that the Board was as yet
far from being the national institution which Butler had
envisioned in his prophetic and imaginative mind. But
at least it was in operation, and it now remained to be
seen how many colleges would find its product acceptable for their purposes.

Through the courtesy of Columbia University and its
president, Seth Low, ample and convenient offices for
the Board had been provided in the library building at
Columbia, and Butler was installed there as secretary.
In the autumn of 1901 President Low resigned in order

to run for the mayoralty. Butler was chosen to succeed him as President of Columbia and naturally had to give up his active association with the Board as its secretary. Nevertheless, on November 9, 1901, he also followed Low as chairman of the College Entrance Examination Board and continued to use his increasingly powerful influence to promote its interests. He served in that capacity until November, 1914.

In his first, and only, report as secretary, Dr. Butler made some significant remarks on the policies of the Board which he had been so instrumental in creating. At one point, he said:

It is quite untrue that the aim of the college admission examination is, primarily, to test the work of the secondary schools. That is merely incidental to its main purpose, which is to ascertain whether a pupil is well enough equipped for more advanced study in college or scientific school.

This observation should be considered in conjunction with an excerpt from an address made by President Arthur T. Hadley, of Yale, in the autumn of 1900, before the New England Association of Colleges and Secondary Schools, in which he declared that college admission examinations should be "tests of the power to take up the work which is to follow rather than tests of past accomplishment merely." Without, perhaps, being fully aware of the implications of what they were saying, both Hadley and Butler were looking forward to a new phase of the examining process, one which was not to develop, however, until some years had passed and teachers were more ready to accept the novel idea.

It was appropriate that Butler, in what was really his "swan song" on the Board, should emphasize what seemed to him to be important. In his report, under date of September 1, 1901, he said:

There are two opposing theories of the college admission examination and of the relations between colleges and schools. According to one theory, widely tho [*sic*] perhaps unconsciously held, the admission examination is a puzzle which the schools are to try to solve. The colleges and schools face each other in June of each year as antagonists, and, on the basis of previous contests, the school prepares itself for each new encounter. It is a logical consequence of this theory that some colleges resent the cooperation of the schools in organizing and conducting the admission examinations, and that some schools bring in special coaches, or "crammers," in April or May of each year, who are supposed to be specially skilled in getting pupils ready to pass the tests prescribed by a given college. While this process is going on, normal education is, of course, suspended.

The other theory of the college admission examination lays less stress upon the examination itself and more upon the pupils and their proper education. It regards the examination as a means, not an end. It follows, therefore, that it is not only wise, but important and highly desirable, that representatives of the secondary schools, who have taught and are teaching the pupils, should confer with representatives of the colleges, who are to teach them, in arranging and enforcing a test the sole purpose of which is to determine whether the pupil is ready to go forward with advantage from the one teacher or institution to the other.

Nobody but a man of Butler's prestige and courage could have spoken out so frankly on the evils of the "cramming" system—a system which undoubtedly operated to a dangerous extent in his time and which, however antiquated, is still behind the opposition to some of the Board's present achievement tests. It has always been hard to convince some teachers that absorbing information in a hurry, even with a damp towel around the forehead, is not the best method of "beating" an examination.

Dr. Butler had this to say in conclusion, regarding the future of the Board:

It is apparent that the principles to which the Association of Colleges and Secondary Schools of the Middle States and Maryland gave its approval when it asked for the formation of the College Entrance Examination Board are as workable in practice as they are sound in theory. The Board has accepted the opportunity that President Eliot pointed out during the discussion that led to its formation, of "making an immense contribution to American education." How immense that contribution might be, perhaps even Mr. Eliot did not fully realize. It includes not only the good results upon colleges and schools of community of interest and community of effort, but it means the breaking down of untold barriers to sound secondary and collegiate education by carrying high and well-defined standards of teaching and of testing into secondary schools, public and private, in every part of the United States. The work of the Board will promptly elevate the secondary school work in English, in history, and in the natural sciences to a new plane of importance and of effectiveness. It will control the examination system in the interest of education, and resist the tendency to make it a mere machine-like performance. It will declare and enforce standards of attainment which represent, not the labors of a zealous individual, however wise, but the mature judgment of a group of mature scholars of different training and points of view.

The secondary school teachers may well be pardoned the unrestrained enthusiasm they have shown at the Board's organization and early work. The experience of each year should enable that work to be improved beyond the risk of fair criticism.

It was fitting that this statement of the hope that lay ahead should come from the person to whom the promising start was chiefly due. Nicholas Murray Butler moved with the new century into a broader life of leadership and usefulness. Other people were to take over the project to which he had devoted so much time and attention. But the stamp of his alert and energizing mind is still on the Board as it continues to function, in somewhat changed form, but with the same aims and ideals, after fifty evolutionary years.

CHAPTER III

THE BOARD
IN ACTION

Considering the fact that nothing of the kind had ever been undertaken before, the previously arranged schedule of the Board examinations in 1901 passed off with a minimum of friction. The 7,889 papers written by the 973 candidates were forwarded from the various centers to New York City, where thirty-nine men and women seated around tables in the Columbia University Library graded them in accordance with a procedure set up in advance. These Readers, appointed May 25, 1901, had been selected, as had the Examiners, with scrupulous care. The Chief Readers included such outstanding figures as Professor George Rice Carpenter, of Columbia, in English, Professor Edwin Seelye Lewis, of Princeton, in French, and Professor Frederick Robertson Jones, of Union, in History. In accordance with the announced policy of the Board, at least one secondary school teacher was included in each group. Some of these, like Emery Winfield Given, of Newark Academy, in Greek, Theodore C. Mitchell, of the Dewitt Clinton High School, in English, and Frederick E. Farrington, of the Collegiate School, in Mathematics, early made themselves felt, as dominant personalities have always done in Board affairs. In the amicable but spirited arguments which developed, the secondary school representatives were too well informed to be ignored.

To ensure some degree of uniformity, the members of each reading group spent preliminary hours establishing workable principles and even in looking over and criticising specimen answer books. The conversation at meals was devoted to informal discussion of problems, relieved by laughter over "boners" which had appeared during the day. These educational pioneers approached their task good-naturedly, with similar ideas and standards and a willingness to co-operate. For them it was both a test and an adventure.

The results on the whole were gratifying. The examination in Chemistry had defects, but that was the only one which was disappointing. Although the comments from the schools indicated that the examinations were regarded as unusually difficult and that the marking was severe, there was little complaint about their fairness. The Secretary pointed out that the one criticism which the Board could not afford to face—namely, that the questions were too easy—was not made. It was apparent that the colleges could have confidence in the new Board. And why not? After all, members of their own faculties had helped to frame the questions!

So far, however, only Columbia, Barnard, and New York University had absolutely abandoned their own examinations in favor of those created by the Board. Harvard, Yale, Princeton, Amherst, and other Eastern colleges continued to set and administer their own tests, as they had done before the Board was organized. Thirty-seven of them promised to allow the Board examinations as substitutes for their own, but Harvard and Bowdoin would not even make this concession. The Harvard faculty, cherishing its traditional independence and not averse to thwarting its President, had voted "with no dissenting voice" that it was inexpedient to accept the proposed certificates of the Board; and Dean Clement L. Smith, in communicating this decision, wrote on January 6, 1901:

The experiment you have entered upon is certainly an important one, and its progress will be watched with much interest; but the fact must be recognized that it is as yet only an experiment, and those of us who have taken an active part in efforts for uniformity in admission requirements are fully aware of the difficulties that stand in the way.

President Hyde, of Bowdoin, equally conservative, wrote to Butler, February 20, 1901:

It does not seem wise to commit ourselves to any system at present, but to reserve our action until it can be made most effective for the extension of the principle among New England institutions.

Butler was frankly disturbed by the failure of two such excellent institutions to sponsor his cherished project; and he was equally annoyed when it appeared that while the Sheffield Scientific School recognized the Board examinations as acceptable substitutes for its own separate tests, Yale College would accept the results of the Board examinations only after the answer books of the candidates concerned had been re-read and re-rated by members of its faculty. Secretary Fiske wrote caustically in 1902: "It is obvious . . . that the careful plan of work adopted by the Board makes it impossible

that any rating assigned by the Board to an answer-boo[
should be materially altered when the book is re-rea[
at Yale College."

Fiske was positive—but he was also right. Everyboo[
now had an opportunity to compare the Board e[
aminations with those of the New York Regents and [
the individual colleges, and the comparison was alt[
gether to the advantage of the Board. Of the papers co[
sidered, 40.7 percent were marked below 60, the grac[
customarily accepted as "passing" by college admissio[
officers. This, in the judgment of experts, was too hig[
a percentage of failure; but at any rate nobody cou[
maintain that the Board had let down the bars. Butl[
commented with some satisfaction: "A reading of th[
questions set in the examinations will show, I think, tha[
they are much more thoro [sic], better balanced, an[
more searching than those set by the colleges indivi[
ually."

The papers were not only more scientifically prepare[
but also more discerningly read, as the leading prepar[
tory schools were not slow to perceive. The word wa[
passed around at association meetings that the Boar[
was doing a fine job. Bowdoin College saw the tren[
and on December 7, 1901, was welcomed into the fol[

The first difficult ordeal had been overcome, and [
was clear that the Board was moving towards a co[
siderable expansion. The smaller New England colleg[
and the independent schools had been watching th[
venture with mingled curiosity and hope; and the Ne[
England Association of Colleges and Secondary Schoo[
had gone so far as to appoint a committee headed by i[
alert secretary, Frank A. Hill, to report on a similar pla[

for that section. Encouraged by this evidence of outside interest, the Board, at its annual meeting on November 9, 1901, dropped from its cumbersome title the phrase "of the Middle States and Maryland" and instructed the Chairman and Secretary to invite the colleges and secondary schools of the New England States to send delegates to the Board. Moreover, the New England Association was requested to name five of its members to represent the secondary schools just as soon as five or more New England colleges had joined the Board. Almost immediately the Massachusetts Institute of Technology, Mount Holyoke College, and Wellesley College took favorable action. An editorial in the *Educational Review* for January, 1901, warning that the work of the College Entrance Examination Board had entered upon a "sternly practical phase," went on to strike a note of optimism:

When the New England Board comes into existence, it is not unsafe to predict that the two will unite and form a single body to represent the entire territory east of the Ohio River and north of the Potomac. In time there may be but one such Board for the entire country.

The favorable reception of the first examination results removed any doubt in Butler's mind as to the desirability of sending out feelers on a matter so dear to his heart. Before retiring as secretary he wrote:

The one thing remaining to ensure the permanent success of the Board, and to put its finances on a sound basis, is for the cooperating colleges, including Princeton, to follow the example of Barnard, Columbia, Cornell (after 1901), and New York University, and substitute the Board's examinations absolutely for their own separate admission examinations, now held in June of each year. Until this is done the more timid of the secondary-school teachers will feel that the favor of the colleges may best be sought by directing their pupils to the separate examinations, and this will prolong the very conditions from which schools and colleges alike profess to be so eager to escape.

But even the dynamic Butler could not hurry an educational reform. He could not have been pleased to read in the Board's *Report* for 1902 that while 461 candidates took examinations for Columbia, only 31 took them for admission to Princeton, 14 to Yale, and one lonely soul to Harvard. Clearly more quiet missionary work was necessary. The Constitution was amended on November 7, 1903, to permit four different associations—the New England, the Middle States, the Southern States, and the North Central—to send representatives from secondary schools. In 1904, as indicative of progress, Harvard at last joined the Board for which her President had battled so valiantly, and Western Reserve also became a member. Furthermore, the powerful New England Association sent its own first representative from the preparatory schools, Dr. William Gallagher, who had been headmaster of Thayer Academy, South Braintree, Massachusetts, since 1896; and Dr. Edward L. Harris, of the Central High School, Cleveland, Ohio, appeared to represent the North Central Association. No longer was it possible to speak disparagingly of the Board as insular or sectional. Slowly but surely it was winning respect and gaining ground, as additional institutional members took their seats. Williams College joined in 1907, Smith College in 1907, Dartmouth College and Wesleyan University in 1908. Yale, more cautious, did not take the decisive step until 1909; while Princeton and Amherst, still less daring, waited until 1910. By that date the stability and success of the Board were no longer in doubt.

It must not be overlooked, however, that although the superior quality of the Board's examinations was gradually being conceded by the schools, most Eastern colleges still continued to set and administer their own tests also—a discouraging waste, it would seem, of energy, time, money, and professional intelligence. The Secretary was pained because as late as 1911—a decade after the Board's foundation—the number of candidates examined by Harvard, Yale, Princeton, Pennsylvania, Bryn Mawr, Stevens, and the Massachusetts Institute of Technology was still in the aggregate larger than the number registering with the Board.

The experience of the first few months had indicated that the Board could function efficiently only with a secretary who could devote much of his time to its business; and the prestige of Dr. Butler made the choice of his successor particularly important. It was Butler himself who persuaded Professor Thomas Scott Fiske, of the Columbia Department of Mathematics, that he should accept the position, and at the Board meeting in the autumn of 1901, he was duly elected. He was to remain as secretary for thirty-five years, throughout controversies and vicissitudes.

Professor Fiske, then in his late thirties, was already a mathematician of distinction. In 1888, with three fellow-students at Columbia and two of the faculty, he helped to organize the New York Mathematical Society and became its first secretary. This expanded in 1894 into the American Mathematical Society, with Fiske still the driving force in the organization. In 1899 he was a leader in establishing the *Transactions of the American Mathematical Society,* a journal for the publication of original investigations in that field, and two years later he was made its editor. He was also the first editor of the *Bulletin of the American Mathematical Society.* Meanwhile he had been appointed professor of Mathematics in Columbia University. On September 7, 1938, at the Fiftieth Anniversary of the American Mathematical Society, Dr. Frederick C. Ferry presented to the society a portrait of Dr. Fiske, by Mrs. Ogden Campbell, together with a beautifully illuminated testimonial, reading in part:

The American Mathematical Society on its Fiftieth Anniversary greets with particular affection and esteem the man in whose mind its organization first took shape. Various members of the Society have shared its purposes, problems, and achievements from its earliest days to the present, none more vitally than he. As Secretary, Editor, and President, as well as in other offices of responsibility, he has supplemented initiative with long-continued service and devotion. . . . The Society would like to believe that its Founder may be justly proud of its accomplishments, as it takes pride in his and addresses to him this testimony of grateful regard as with him it sets its face towards the future.

What Fiske was like as a personality and administrator will become more clear as this narrative proceeds. He moved easily through tables of statistics, reaching conclusions before his associates trained in the Classics or in History had been able to resuscitate their almost moribund acquaintance with arithmetic. Indeed, he had a professional passion for assembling and interpreting formidable rows of figures. Until age slowed him down, he was a sensitive scholar, quick to apprehend the direction of contemporary scientific thought. Naturally shy and self-conscious, he found it difficult to mix with others, and deliberately stayed away from committee luncheons in order that his associates might feel free to discuss his work. Erect and handsome, fashionably garbed in a cutaway coat and striped trousers, with hair which changed gradually from gray to pure white, he moved slowly and impressively through any assemblage and confronted crises with nonchalant ease. He had little sense of humor or of proportion, and as he grew older was inclined to dwell at inordinate length on the early history of any question brought to his attention. At times he showed himself deficient in imagination and flexibility. But he was a tireless worker, and his attention to details inspired confidence in his opinions. His background, temperament, and devotion to duty made him an ideal secretary, especially during the Board's formative period. "Its welfare," writes Dr. Frederick C. Ferry, "was his chief ambition in life."

Butler was, of course, still chairman of the Board and spent with it as much time as he could spare from the manifold interests which claimed his attention. Fiske is not to be compared with a genius like Butler, but he did possess distinctive virtues of his own, among them patience (which was not one of Butler's attributes), persistence, and tact. He did not often originate ideas, but he was no obstructionist. It was his undramatic task to keep the office running day after day—to create a clearing house of information available to anybody concerned with educational problems. Describing his duties as he saw them after a few months, he said that they involved internal correspondence with examiners and readers, external correspondence with candidates and teachers, and the constant preparation of pamphlets and bulletins. He also had to offer advice, to settle disputes, and to some extent to decide minor matters of policy—a little cautiously at first, but later with assurance. He knew better than anyone else except Butler how necessary it was to convince both colleges and schools that the Board was from them indispensable.

Fiske was well aware that he must be for some years a glorified salesman for his employers. In his first *Report,* published on September 1, 1902, he seized the opportunity to pay a tribute to the representatives of secondary education; and his statement of the basic aims of the Board was as emphatic as anything that Butler had written:

The chief aim of the College Entrance Examination Board is to secure, by means of cooperation between all those vitally interested, that uniformity of standards which is essential for the general systematic improvement of the conditions of secondary education. . . . In every important problem that affects the relations between the college and the secondary school, the judgment of those who have achieved for themselves eminence in the world of secondary education is at least of equal importance with the judgment of those who have attained similar distinction in the college world. . . . It would not be surprising to the writer if it should turn out eventually that the general acceptance of the principles and standards for which the Board stands will be due even more to the influence of the secondary schools than to that of the colleges.

Remarks of this tenor may seem suspiciously like "flattering unction," deliberately prepared to soothe the ruffled feelings of schoolmasters who feared that the Board, or some of its members, had as their half-concealed desire the dictation of policies from above. But some such assurance was needed. Schools are always sensitive on this point, just as certain states, especially those which are small or isolated, have been jealous of their autonomy and need reiterated assurance. One member of the Headmasters' Association is reported to have muttered, "I'll be damned if any Board down in New York City, with a college professor at its head, is going to tell me and my faculty what or how to teach!" Against prejudices and eruptions of this sort Professor Fiske, possibly a little troubled by his exclusively collegiate background, had to use soft words and mild persuasion. It would have been fatal if he had shown any traces of superciliousness.

On the other hand, he could be, when necessary, disarmingly frank. Commenting on the fact that some higher institutions were finding it advantageous to adopt different passing marks for different subjects, he made it clear that local conditions would probably induce numerous colleges to accept for awhile, and in a few fields, lower ratings than they would eventually demand. To put it plainly, the Board marking, decided upon by men and women outstanding in their profession, was often too strict for colleges which had been accustomed to select applicants from a lower level of preparation. As Fiske put the matter, this was probably inevitable, at least until the instruction in certain schools had improved; but he added that under the plan adopted by the Board, it was possible for any institution "to exercise discretion."

One unexpected issue arose early from the complaint of some suspicious schoolmasters that it was unfair to have secondary school instructors serving on the committees of examiners for subjects which they themselves were teaching in the classroom, the implication being that such instructors could favor their own pupils by giving them the special drill and knowledge which would enable them better to answer the questions on the paper. This astonishing reflection by teachers on the integrity of their fellow-craftsmen met with a quick and well-deserved rebuke. In his 1901 *Report,* Butler published comments from seven representatives of preparatory schools, declaring that any such violation of professional ethics was inconceivable in a group of such high reputation. Frank Rollins, Associate Examiner in Physics, summarized his reaction in a single sentence: "I cannot believe that any teacher whom you would be likely to select for this work would be seriously embarrassed or would permit himself or his pupils to derive any advantage from his connection with the preparation of the examination."

My own personal acquaintance with examiners has confirmed a conviction that they have been exceptionally careful to avoid any unethical use of their necessarily intimate and confidential knowledge of the questions. No similar charges were made after the first year of the Board's operations.

The experience of those first crucial months taught

everybody—members, examiners, and readers—a great deal. In preliminary conferences the Readers developed more effective techniques. Their judgments in some fields, such as English and History, could hardly escape being subjective, but every paper marked originally below 60 percent was reread and often discussed at length. Fallibility was thus reduced to a minimum, and the correlation with later grades in the colleges seemed to improve from season to season.

For the second year, Spanish, Botany, Geography, and Drawing were added, by request, to the list of subjects. The examinations were rendered more completely impersonal by the assignment of numbers to the candidates. In 1902 examinations were held at 130 centers and administered to 1,362 candidates—an increase of exactly 40 percent. One hundred and forty public schools furnished 30 percent of the registrants, and the private schools represented numbered 248. The largest single group came from the Sachs Collegiate Institute, in New York City.

Statistics confirm the impression that for almost a decade the Board was implemented for the Middle Atlantic States, including New York. In 1901 the candidates included 814 from the Middle States as against 101 from the South and the West and only 48 from New England. Five years later the records showed 1,489 from the Middle States, 464 from the South and the West, and 457 from New England. The Yankees were evidently doing slightly better. In 1910 the tests were taken by 3,731 boys and girls, of whom 1,129 resided in New England, 1,626 were attending New England schools, and 1,968 wished to attend New England colleges. For the first time, the Secretary announced, the number examined in New England was larger than the number from the Middle States. It is significant also that up to 1908 the largest number from any one institution came from New York City schools. In that year, however, St. Paul's School, Concord, New Hampshire, took the lead, and in 1910 the largest delegation came from the Phillips Exeter Academy. Figures such as these may be interpreted as indicating that the Board was widening its scope and making an impression on even the more conservative educators. In 1913 the candidates choosing a New England college numbered 2,067, as compared with 1,493 selecting colleges in the Middle States and 113 those in the South. By this date the New England colleges needed no further demonstration; indeed, their representatives were becoming more and more active in the Board's affairs, and all their doubts had been resolved.

The most important step taken by the Board in those early days was the creation of the Committee of Review. The Founders of the Board had tacitly assumed that it should not be responsible for framing requirements in the various subjects, but should rely on such scholarly bodies as the Modern Language Association and the National Committee on College Entrance Requirements. As it turned out, many, if not most, of these organizations had only a slight interest in secondary school teaching, and soon the Board found itself virtually compelled to set its own standards. Its Constitution was, therefore, amended in 1907 to authorize the Chairman to appoint a Committee of Review consisting of seven members, three of them from preparatory schools. The first members were Dean Hurlbut, of Harvard (chairman); President Taylor, of Vassar; Dean Crane, of Cornell; Dean Ferry, of Williams; Mr. Farrand, of Newark Academy; Mr. Gallagher, of Thayer Academy; and Mr. Harris, of the Central High School, of Cleveland. It was supposedly the function of this committee to follow continuously from year to year the practical working of the requirements in each subject and to make arrangements for their modification whenever that seemed to be desirable. Actually it adopted the procedure of asking special commissions of school and college teachers to study particular fields, such as Botany or Spanish, and give their expert advice. When one of these commissions had formulated its conclusions, its recommendations were submitted to critical opinion throughout the country. As a final step, these were passed upon by the full Board as a report from the Committee of Review.

With such a mandate and with such sweeping powers, the Committee of Review soon became a paramount factor in the evolution of the secondary school curriculum, with a salutary influence on both subject matter and teaching methods. Secretary Fiske had noted in 1902 what he thought to be a tendency for some schools to adopt the Board examinations as a means of testing the fitness of their candidates for graduation, but this never moved beyond the preliminary stage. Reputable schools, like colleges, have always preferred to accept the judgments of their own faculty members. The establishment of definite Board requirements for entrance examinations, however, did have a direct effect on all schools concerned with keeping up high standards, for they could now learn how their own work checked with that of their rivals and, if necessary, could change their methods. For example, the Committee of Review soon turned its attention to the examinations in Physics and in History—two subjects which had been causing a vast amount of trouble. At its suggestion, the Board requested the American Historical Association to undertake a sweeping revision of the requirement in History. Professor E. D. Fite, of Vassar College, Chief Reader in History, made in 1914 a most illuminating report, demonstrating that the preparation for the Board's examinations in that subject was extraordinarily and ridiculously uneven. In a masterly use of understatement, he said:

Inasmuch as the standard to which the examination questions are made to conform requires daily work for a year in each subject, satisfactory results cannot reasonably be expected from those candidates who have devoted to their subject short recitation periods, two or three times a week, for only a part of the year.

In 1914 only 32 percent of all the candidates in American History received a rating of 60 or better, and in Medieval and Modern History the record was even worse. Clearly something was wrong somewhere, and the Committee of Review, after its survey, concluded that inadequate preparation was the commonest cause of failure. Before long even good schools found it necessary to reorganize their curricula in order to assign more time to History. In this instance, as in several others, the Board accomplished what could never have been done through any other instrumentality. Teachers of History in schools with inadequate standards learned, by attending conferences of Readers, what were their own deficiencies—and often quietly remedied them. Furthermore, a large number of colleges gradually altered their requirements for admission in History to bring them into conformity with the definitions adopted by the Board.

In some nations and at some periods uniformity in education has undoubtedly been pressed too far. Regimentation like that in Fascist Germany or even in the state schools of democratic France can submerge individualism and deny pupils the privilege of expressing their personalities. But individualism in American schools in the 1900's had so far run riot that the establishment of a uniform standard of excellence had become not only desirable but even obligatory if a close articulation between school and college was to be retained. The Committee of Review, entirely independent of any state bureaucracy and with no power to enforce regulations, presented an ideal towards which schools and schoolmasters could move without sacrificing any of their much-prized freedom. Inspiration thus accomplished what compulsion could never have done.

Another medium for the achievement of a beneficial uniformity was the Committee on Examination Ratings, authorized in 1910. The "Art of Examination"— to borrow the title of one of President A. Lawrence Lowell's most thoughtful essays—was then little understood, and even misunderstood, and the early groups of Readers revealed amazing whims and prejudices which they were reluctant to abandon, if only because of personal or institutional pride. It was the business of this new committee to bring the Readers to a broader conception of their responsibility and to convert them painlessly to certain philosophical principles by which they could be guided. Once again, it was for the Readers a matter of subordinating individual preferences to the general good of the educational community—a lesson which they were not slow to learn.

This Committee on Examination Ratings, after a thorough study of conditions, reported, in April, 1911, some of its findings: that many of the questions set by the Examiners had really been too difficult; that the answer books proved that some students had been poorly taught; that a considerable number of girls and boys had "taken a chance" at tests which they were clearly unfitted to pass; and that one reason for low marks was to be found in the high percentage of weak students who, not being able to secure certificates from their schools, had taken the Board's examinations as a forlorn hope. The committee recommended to the Board that the Chief Reader in each subject be given more authority to make decisions on matters of policy; that all the Chief Readers meet in conference each year before beginning their marking to discuss procedures; and finally that Readers be encouraged to use discretion and grade papers "according to a standard of fairness and common sense, rather than on a strictly mechanical basis."

The appointment of these two powerful committees showed to the outside public that the Board was very far from being like Old Jim Jay, who "got stuck fast in yesterday." It was watching Argus-eyed for defects in its own machinery; it was looking for and making use of helpful talent wherever it could be uncovered; it was friendly towards experimentation and research. Its willingness to assume leadership was becoming more apparent.

One illustration will show how the system worked. In 1913 Professor Fiske devoted considerable space in his annual report to the efforts which had been made to secure a revision of the requirements in Chemistry—a field in which changes had been rapid and comprehensive. The Board referred the problem to the Committee of Review, which in turn appointed a commission of seven members. Professor Alexander Smith, of Columbia, a distinguished chemist, was designated as chairman, in accordance with the policy of naming a college teacher to preside. When finally selected, the Commission comprised four college professors and three secondary school instructors. As the members were widely separated geographically, the preliminary investigation was carried on largely by correspondence. A full meeting was then held in New York City, with sessions extending to more than twelve hours, as a result of which certain propositions were unanimously approved and an outline of a new requirement was drafted. This statement, slightly modified by the Chairman and Secretary of the Board, was approved by all the members of the Commission and handed on to the Committee of Review, which sent it out to various colleges for further study and comment. The final recommendation of the Committee of Review—the product of many minds in co-operation—was adopted *in toto* by the Board in April, 1913, and published in Document No. 62, issued on the following December 1. The entire procedure, while none too speedy, gave full opportunity for the consideration and evaluation of conflicting ideas; and the result, while in some respects a compromise, met with general approval.

The press was kept busy printing numerous informatory documents prepared in the offices of the Board. A volume of examination questions appeared in September, 1902, containing the 42 papers for the year, together with the names of Examiners and Readers. The Secretary superintended the editing of many Bulletins of Information. As an example, Document No. 12 contained a definition of the requirement in each examination subject for June, 1903, together with the plan of organization of the Board, a list of examination subjects, the names of the Examiners appointed to frame the questions for use in 1903, the schedule of examinations, instructions to candidates and teachers, and a preliminary list of examination centers. The Board, in fact, quickly developed into a complicated organism, involving a vast amount of undramatic but essential administrative detail. Professor Fiske, with his passion for order, enjoyed simplifying tables of statistics and triumphing over confusion.

Practical considerations often led to modifications of policy. In 1910 the Board amended its Constitution to provide that the designations Excellent, Good, Doubtful, Poor, and Very Poor be dropped from the ratings 100–90, 89–75, 74–60, 49–40, and below 40, respectively. It had at first been taken for granted, in accordance with current procedure in 1901, that 60 was a "passing" grade. Many of the members, however, as they watched the evolution of the Board's examination system, reached the conclusion that ratings of 50 might safely be accepted as a guarantee of future respectable college work. This was evidence that some colleges were concluding that the Board tests were not only more just, but also more difficult, than those which they had been setting. At last a criterion was available by which a college, if it so desired, could measure itself against other institutions on the same level.

In 1906 the Board initiated the practice of indicating for each subject the highest rating given by the readers to an answer book, and also naming the schools whose students earned this distinction. In that year it appeared that grades of 100 were awarded in Latin Grammar to 2; in Latin Composition to 1; in Elementary Algebra to 20; in Algebra to Quadratics to 12; in Plane Geometry to 33; in Solid Geometry to 2; in Plane and Solid Geometry to 2; in Physics to 1; and in Drawing to 2. These revelations, as they gained publicity, resulted in a poorly-veiled competition between schools, and even between teachers, and were eventually discontinued as serving no useful purpose. Readers in History and English announced that in those subjects there could be no such phenomenon as a "perfect" paper; and when in 1917 one lonely candidate was rated 100 in American History, the effect was sensational. Unfortunately I have been unable to discover the name of this genius or his record in later life. In the 1920's grades of 100 were awarded even in the Comprehensive English examination, one of the first being granted to Eugene V. Rostow, afterwards the leader of his class at Yale and now a Professor in Yale Law School.

Butler never abandoned the hope that the Board, even though not aiming directly at that goal, might raise the standards of American secondary schools. Fiske followed the same course so far as he deemed it expedient to do so, keeping in mind always the danger of making unwise comparisons or injuring the feelings of sensitive headmasters. The Board could never have announced bluntly that it intended to improve the secondary schools. That would have brought a swarm of pedagogical hornets around Professor Fiske's head. But indirectly it did achieve its unavowed purpose. Wilson Farrand, himself a headmaster, speaking as late as 1925, declared:

The great need of the secondary schools of today is the establishment of adequate standards of attainment. Their great weakness is sloppiness and superficiality; their great need is thoroughness and genuine mastery of the subjects taught. It is my deliberate conviction that the strongest factor in the improvement of our secondary schools in the last twenty-five years is to be found in the standards set and maintained by forward and upward-looking teachers through the agency of the College Entrance Examination Board.

Throughout these exciting educational developments, the officials of the Board could not escape the sordid exigencies of the budget. Theoretically the infant Board had behind it the resources of its parent colleges; nevertheless, it had its share of financial embarrassments. The original Treasurer, Joseph C. Hendrix, President of the National Bank of Commerce, was a friend of Dr. Butler and had accepted the position as purely nominal, turning over the accounting to a subordinate. In 1905 Professor Fiske was elected both Secretary and Treasurer, combining two offices. The actual running expenses during the first year of operation were less than $6,000, but it will be recalled that Butler accepted no salary as Secretary and that the Board paid no rental for its headquarters. No one could have complained that it was making a splurge. Dr. Butler was allowed to engage as Assistant Secretary, Dr. William W. Waters, formerly President of Wells College, who was paid $2,000 and attended to the routine and miscellaneous correspondence. The first Chairman, Seth Low, was an admirable presiding officer, deliberate and courteous, with an unfailing supply of anecdotes to relieve the tedium of dull meetings—but he did very little except preside. Even the usually dynamic Vice-Chairman, President M. Carey Thomas, of Bryn Mawr, was content to watch matters from a distance, giving an occasional commendatory nod or word. The earliest Executive Committee consisted of the Chairman (Dr. Low), the Vice-Chairman (Miss Thomas), together with President James M. Taylor, of Vassar, Professor William A Lamberton, of the University of Pennsylvania, and Dr. Julius Sachs. It was Butler, however, who held the reins and guided the chariot of the Board.

In Butler's Report for the first year he estimated that at least $6,000 annually would be required to carry on the normal work of the Board as it was then functioning. Like an old-fashioned pump, the Board had to be "primed" before its revenue would start to flow, and a generous anonymous friend, presumably Butler himself, advanced $3,500 to get it under way for the first fiscal year. On May 18, 1901, Butler requested each co-operating college to make a contribution, and his appeal met with a gratifying response. Nevertheless, the Board had ahead of it a period of "hard trials and great tribulation." The *Second Annual Report* revealed the sad news that the Board was "in the red" to the amount of $6,800. As time went on, costs steadily mounted, while the income, although rising, did not accelerate correspondingly. Professor Fiske must often have recalled Mr. Micawber's famous definition of the difference between happiness and misery: "Annual income twenty pounds, annual expenditure nineteen nineteen six, result happiness. Annual income twenty pounds, annual expenditure twenty pounds ought and six, result misery."

Fortunately his serenity, even when the books could not be made to balance, kept up the spirits of his associates.

Some figures will show what was happening. In 1904 the running expenses were about $10,000, while the revenue, chiefly from examination fees, was $9,883. In 1908 the disbursements were $18,452 and the receipts $17,363. By 1910, the gap had widened, with the expenditures aggregating $23,221.15 and the income $20,130. In any business the impulse of the directors would have been to change the management. Things had grown even worse by 1915, when the expenses were $31,335.46 and the total income $26,090—leaving out entirely $2,102.83 expended for the replacement of documents and furniture destroyed by fire in the offices of the Board. In 1917 the situation became really serious, for the cost of operation for the year was $61,884.67, and the receipts from all sources added up to only $47,467.50. While the Board was not in business for financial profit, it was evident that it could not long resist collapse when it was losing $15,000 annually.

Luckily the Carnegie Corporation, through Butler's influence, came to the rescue with a subvention of $7,500. At the same time the Board itself took a step which had been too long delayed and raised the examination fee from $5 to $6, explaining that this action was necessitated "by the increased cost of such services as are essential to the successful conduct of the Board's work and the establishment of the comprehensive examinations." In this connection it is worth noting that the cost per candidate had risen from $.95 in 1901 to $1.79 in 1905, and was advancing every year. The Secretary was not a good prophet when he wrote in 1904—"There can be no doubt that the work of the Board is rapidly advancing to a self-supporting basis." How could it possibly support itself when the candidates were not paying the bare cost of the service which they were receiving?

In 1921, during the postwar inflation, the Board seemed again to be moving irretrievably towards disaster, with a deficit for the year of $24,019.54. Authority was hastily granted to the Treasurer to borrow up to $30,000 to meet contingencies; and the Board wisely, although with much regret, raised the fee from $6 to $9. In commenting on this drastic action, Secretary Fiske said:

That the work of the College Entrance Examination Board must be supported by the examination fees becomes more and more obvious as the work of the Board expands. . . . The fees received last June fell short of meeting the Board's expenses by more than $35,000. The Board reached and passed the limits imposed by its resources and was compelled to seek financial assistance in order to meet its immediate necessities and to continue its operations. . . .

It is to be expected that there will be many protests against the increase in the examination fee and that some of the protests will be significant of a real hardship resulting to candidates of slender means. Most of them, however, will manifest the disinclination of the American public in matters educational to pay full value for what they receive, a spirit engendered by the habit of getting something for nothing or for a small part at most of its real cost.

Professor Fiske's cynicism, although doubtless justified by his experience with disgruntled parents, was not borne out by events. Protests were few and feeble, and the number taking the examinations continued during the 1920's to increase. Meanwhile, in 1920 the Constitution of the Board had been amended to authorize the appointment of three Custodians, to control the property held by or for the Board. For some years the Custodians had little money to guard or invest; but in 1925, in the Coolidge Golden Age, the receipts at last exceeded the expenditures, $203,965.92 against $186,707.21. After a quarter of a century of financial uncertainty, the Board was in the pleasing situation of having a respectable surplus. This did wonders to the morale of the officers, who could at last afford the luxury of research and expansion, and strengthened their administrative self-respect. From that day to the present the Board has been able to maintain a reserve fund for emergencies by the simple expedient, familiar to industry, of charging the customers enough to ensure a modest profit. The importance of a financial backlog has been demonstrated again and again in the recent history of the Board.

Controlled at first by Butler, the Board soon ceased to be a one-man organization, but grew into a democratic body of strong and diverse personalities, some of them fertile in ideas and all of them accustomed to campus leadership. No group which included such college presidents as William H. P. Faunce, of Brown, Miss Ellen Fitz Pendleton, of Wellesley, Miss Mary E. Woolley, of Mount Holyoke, Charles F. Thwing, of Western Reserve, and Miss M. Carey Thomas, of Bryn Mawr, was likely to be docile or inarticulate; and the secondary school contingent, headed by Julius Sachs and Wilson Farrand, could hold their own with anybody. Meeting intimately around a table, they measured one another's capacity and sense of humor and broadened their outlook.

In a study of this scope it is impossible to do justice to everybody who shared the responsibility. Among those who commanded the most respect was Professor Robert N. Corwin, who had been an outstanding football player at Yale in the 1880's and later, as chairman of that university's Committee on Admission, persuaded it to join the Board in 1909 and was its first representative there, serving actively until his retirement from the Yale faculty in 1934. A Long Islander by birth, but a Yankee by heritage and temperament, he combined a keen, mature, and analytical mind with the heart of a boy. His understanding of human nature was profound, and without any instruction from books he knew how to win friends and influence people. In his childhood he had been taught a thrifty economy, which led him later, as a member of the Board's Finance Committee and one of its Custodians, to scrutinize every expenditure. He was far from parsimonious, but he had learned to avoid waste in days when, as Dean Heermance has expressed it, "it was an achievement to vote the annual budget, and a comprehensive motion to spend thousands of dollars would have created a minor earthquake." Corwin was a member of the Committee of Review for eighteen years and its chairman for fifteen, and he was elected and re-elected to the Executive Committee for eighteen consecutive terms. He was also a Custodian for almost a decade. A delightful fragment of autobiography, published after his death by his wife under the quaint title, *The Plain Unpolished Tale of the Workaday Doings of Modest Folk,* reveals the whimsical humor, the physical and mental robustness, and the rich philosophy of a remarkable man. He has been accurately characterized by a colleague as "suave, keen, and forceful, puncturing innumerable bubbles with his innocent, impertinent, and irreverent questions." He and Nicholas Murray Butler were elected honorary members-at-large of the Board in October, 1934, but he continued to attend meetings as an Elder Statesman until just before his death ten years later.

Another extraordinarily useful member for many years was Frederick C. Ferry, a Vermonter by birth and a Williams graduate who later became Dean of that College (1902–17) and then President of Hamilton College (1917–38). His association with the Board began in 1906. A small-college man, he could match wits successfully with the representatives of universities and not only served with them on important committees but also helped on more than one occasion to rewrite the

Board's Constitution. He became the wise Ulysses of the Board, who could say with pride:

> Much have I seen and known; cities of men
> And manners, climates, councils, governments,
> Myself not least, but honor'd of them all.

A gentleman of quiet dignity and personal charm, Dr. Ferry has been a welcome father confessor to his juniors on the Board, and his spicy and salty reminiscences of the "good old days" have delighted the historian. He, too, was elected an honorary member-at-large in 1943, in recognition of his distinguished record on the Board.

Following the First World War, a new group of leaders, including Dean Howard McClenahan, of Princeton, Professor Adam Leroy Jones, of Columbia, Dr. Henry Pennypacker, of Harvard, President William A. Neilson, of Smith, and others, became prominent in the Board's affairs. They belong more appropriately in a later chapter, along with Miss Mary E. Woolley, the first woman to be chosen Chairman.

In 1914 President Butler formally resigned as Chairman of the College Entrance Examination Board. More and more he had been widening his activities, and in 1912 had even run for the Vice-Presidency on the Republican ticket headed by the ill-fated William H. Taft. He perceived also that the Board had reached a stage when his sponsorship was no longer indispensable to its prosperity. In his valedictory he spoke out with his usual refreshing frankness.

It is certain that much remains to be done before college admissions will be perfect; but the College Entrance Examination Board has shown that these examinations may be so improved and their effect upon secondary school instruction made so stimulating, that for a college to maintain separate admission examinations of its own is surely a mark either of weakness, or of perversity, or of mere parochialism, or of the stubborn persistence of educational inertia.

In view of the fact that in 1914 Harvard, Yale, Princeton, Amherst, and many other not altogether obscure institutions were continuing to set and administer their own examinations—although accepting those given by the Board—Butler's remarks were a thunderous blast from Manhattan. Nobody seems to have resented his bluntness, however, and within two years most of the outsiders were safe within the fold.

In concluding his farewell address, Butler expressed himself optimistically regarding the future.

If the Board is able, as I confidently believe it will be, to proceed for another decade on its present lines, it will have brought about everywhere a new spirit of comity and cooperation between secondary school and college teachers, and a new and very helpful understanding of the problems which attend the training of boys and girls who are about to be graduated from secondary schools.

The Board, at its next meeting, paid Dr. Butler the tribute he so fully merited, and adopted appropriate resolutions reading in part as follows:

To him is due the conception of the Board. His eloquent advocacy of his plan before educational bodies prepared the way for its organization. His steady guidance, clearness of statement, resolution in holding to the original design, his maintenance of the importance of a dignified and solid basis of membership, and his wisely progressive conservatism in so enlarging the scope of the Board's work as to make it responsive to the needs of the schools and colleges, have laid broad and deep the foundations of the success already achieved. As a presiding officer he has been prompt, courteous, well poised, eminently fair, and effective. For this leadership and for the hospitality of Columbia University, extended through him to the Board in various ways, we are under lasting obligation.

Butler's successor as Chairman was Byron Satterlee Hurlbut, Dean of Harvard College from 1902 to 1916 and Professor of English from 1906 until his death in 1929. A man of liberal views, he supported President Eliot in his enthusiasm for the College Entrance Examination Board and finally through his persuasive powers converted a majority of the Harvard faculty to his opinion. On November 12, 1904, he appeared as Harvard's first representative to the Board meetings. From May 11, 1907, until November 9, 1913, he was the first chairman of the very important Committee of Review and helped to determine its procedure. He was a very efficient Chairman of the Board when he took over in 1914. Wilson Farrand once spoke admiringly of his "genial humanity and deferential modesty, always pretending to be following the lead of some one else, while in reality driving his team with consummate skill." Butler had been positive, assertive, audacious; Hurlbut was addicted to penetrating side-remarks, full of undertones and implications. Butler was imperious; Hurlbut was not disposed to dictate. Perhaps it was just as well that Dr. Butler was followed by somebody so different from himself.

Speaking at the twenty-fifth anniversary of the College Entrance Examination Board, Dr. Henry S. Pritchett, President of the Carnegie Foundation for the Advancement of Teaching, mentioned two qualities of the work of the Board which had placed all agencies of education in our country under a debt of obligation to it. The first was its contribution to the improvement of the written examination "through the labors of a group of mature scholars of varied training who have approached the study of the examination paper from many points of view." The second, and perhaps even more significant contribution, was "its steady exposition of the ideal of sincerity in education." The Board from its inception had maintained honest standards, upheld ethical practices, striven to bring teachers of all types and aims together for the common good. Refusing to accept tradition blindly, it had relied upon experimentation and research. It had made some mistakes—none of them irreparable—and had met with some disappointments. But by 1915 it had won confidence as an instrument for good in American education.

CHAPTER IV

THE MOVE TOWARDS COMPREHENSIVE EXAMINATIONS

Dᴜʀɪɴɢ ᴛʜᴇ sᴇᴄᴏɴᴅ decade of the twentieth century momentous changes were taking place in the thinking of persons interested in the philosophy of examinations, especially those for admission to college. All of a sudden, like the victims of an epidemic, teachers began to pontificate glibly about "comprehensive examinations"—by which they meant examinations not based mainly on the memorization of mastery of assigned subject matter, but rather designed to test a candidate's ability to reason independently and to compare and correlate the material of a broad field of study. President A. Lawrence Lowell, of Harvard, in his essay entitled "The Art of Examination" published in the *Atlantic Monthly* for January, 1926, summed up this new doctrine as follows:

A knowledge of the facts is a small part of education. We hear much today of teaching by problems; and rightly, because bare facts are of little value unless one knows how to use them. The important thing is to understand their relation to one another; to be able to correlate them, as the current expression goes; not merely to grasp and retain the relations one has been taught, but to perceive new relations, for no teacher can cover more than a minor fraction of the combinations actually met in the pursuit of any subject. The pupil must learn to apply principles to new and unexpected situations, and the extent to which he can do so will largely determine the degree of his future effectiveness.

Speaking more specifically, the proponents of the "comprehensive" examinations declared that in the foreign languages, both ancient and modern, emphasis should be laid on sight translation, and in mathematics, on "originals"—on exercises demanding something besides the ability to echo an instructor's demonstrations. They wanted a formula, as accurate and simple as possible, for measuring mental power. President Eliot, that voyager "through strange seas of thought alone," had anticipated many of these advanced ideas. The so-called "Progressives" also claimed some of the credit—and with much justification. The Progressives have always been like the Populist Party—ahead of their generation with theories which have later been borrowed, often without assigning credit, by conservatives.

The idea of comprehensive examinations did at first seem revolutionary and was attacked as such by reactionaries. It disturbed good teachers who had been accustomed to study the Board's bound volumes of old examinations and then "guess" what passages or problems were likely to appear on the next series. Some of them had developed an uncanny gift of prognostication which had brought them prestige, but was obviously useless in tests of the comprehensive type. But the evolution of modern educational psychology had left this method of teaching far in the rear, indeed had made it obsolete. What was once frowned upon as "radicalism" had by 1915 become plain common sense.

Some colleges were going even further by hinting that applicants really needed to be examined in only four broad areas instead of in eight or ten restricted subjects. In mathematics, for example, it was asserted that one test covering the entire field would be more revealing than several in Algebra, Plane and Solid Geometry, and Trigonometry; and it was plausibly argued that this would offer ample opportunity for the display of imagination and resourcefulness. President Lowell, in the *Atlantic* article just mentioned, declared that the quality most important to cultivate in mature students was "the ability to analyze a complex body of facts, to disentangle the essential factors, to grasp their meaning and perceive their relations to one another." This was regarded by headmasters as too much to expect from boys and girls of seventeen or eighteen; but the ultimate aim of all education has seldom been more clearly expressed.

Even the stanchest advocates of comprehensive examinations did not at first contend that they were desirable for everybody, but shrewdly opened their campaign by asserting that such tests would be most valid with brighter students. This led to the theory that there might well be two plans for admission to college—one for exceptionally talented candidates, the other for those who, for want of a better adjective, might be called "average." For this frank differentiation between the sheep and the goats there was much to be said. By 1914 Harvard, led by Dean Hurlbut, with the unflagging support of President Lowell, had put the weight of its prestige behind what was shortly to be called the "New Plan."

Meanwhile a collegiate miracle was taking place. Representatives of Harvard, Yale, and Princeton had been conferring for some years at Board gatherings, with the result that many of the former jealousies and suspicions were disappearing and they were now ready to present a common front. Now Messrs. Hurlbut, Corwin, and McClenahan, authorized by their respective institutions, agreed to abolish their own separate examinations and to use in the future exclusively the tests prepared and read by the Board. This was accomplished only after a heroic struggle with the calendars of the three universities, for each had been using a different system for fixing the beginning and the end of the college year. Professor Fiske, in his *Report* for 1915, wrote in a triumphal strain:

The end of the year saw the virtual achievement of the primary purpose for which the Board was established, the abolishment substantially of the entrance examinations held every June by individual colleges acting independently of one another.

A further step towards uniformity was taken in July, 1915, when at a conference held in New Haven and attended by representatives of Harvard, Yale, Princeton, and the College Entrance Examination Board it was agreed that the Board should prepare, print, and distribute question papers for use in September by those colleges and scientific schools which might be able to agree upon uniform dates for their autumn entrance examinations. Professor Fiske asserted at the time that the complete success of uniform examinations in June depended upon the adoption of uniform examinations in September. An examination schedule for the autumn was shortly put into effect, but the colleges themselves for some years conducted the tests and graded the papers, largely because of the difficulty of getting teachers from the schools to act as Readers during that busy period.

At the conferences which drew Harvard, Yale, and Princeton jointly into closer relationship with the Board the matter of comprehensive examinations was frequently brought up and discussed. In April, 1915, the Board passed resolutions providing that a set of comprehensive examinations should be offered "adapted to the use of those colleges which offer, or propose to offer, comprehensive examinations for admission purposes." Separate committees of Examiners and Readers were authorized to prepare and grade the answer books of the two systems of examinations. As originally passed, these resolutions were intended to provide service primarily for Harvard and any other colleges which might request it. In response to many inquiries, John G. Hart, chairman of the Harvard Committee on Admission, prepared a memorandum, which was printed in the Secretary's *Report:*

To be most useful, the new comprehensive papers must be adapted:

(1) To such variety of school instruction as exists in the several subjects,—that is, they must not prescribe methods, but must recognize the general principle that the schools determine how they shall teach a subject and that the college tests results or power.

(2) To different stages of training in the subjects for

which they are set,—that is, they must give boys oppor-
tunities to show their power, whether they have had the
minimum or the maximum amount of training given in
school. For example, the papers in French should be so
drawn up as to enable a boy who has had only two years of
French to show that he has as much command over the
language as can be expected from that amount of training;
and they must be similarly useful for the boy who has had
three or four years of French.

In 1919 four women's colleges—Mount Holyoke,
Smith, Vassar, and Wellesley—all of them hitherto sup-
porters of the so-called certificate system of admission,
adopted in its place the Board's examinations, and soon
expressed their preference for the New Plan. As techniques were perfected, the comprehensive examinations
in four basic subjects were considered, not separately,
but together, and in conjunction with the school record
furnished ample material upon which the college judgment could be based. The candidate was to receive no
information as to her grades or credits for separate subjects, but would merely learn from the Admissions Officer whether she had been rejected.

The comprehensive examinations never entirely
superseded the Old Plan; indeed, for a time conver-
sions were few. Nevertheless, as one announcement followed another, the groans from the Old Guard were
distinctly audible on Morningside Heights, where the
offices of the Board were located. Secretary Fiske was
"hounded"—to use his own word—by teachers and
pupils inquiring about the nature of the proposed new
tests. The conservatives were up in arms against the New
Plan, complaining that it would be impossible to pre-

pare students for it under the existing curriculum, that it would be difficult to grade the papers accurately, and that it placed a premium on superficial cleverness, not on thoroughness of preparation. There was a cry that the colleges were "letting down the bars." Sensitive to these comments, the officers of the Board took exceptional pains to select as Examiners men and women of broad vision, with a willingness to co-operate in making the experiment a success.

The comprehensive examinations were a symbol of a shift in educational thought—an evolution from rigidity to flexibility, from narrowness to breadth, from emphasis on content to emphasis on choice. Under the new system the English teacher, instead of being shackled year after year to specified "classics," some of them repugnant to youthful minds, could wander as he pleased in the "realms of gold," even using contemporary essays and biographies to interest his pupils. I can remember feeling a sense of liberation as I was left free to teach other Shakesperian plays besides *The Merchant of Venice* and *Macbeth,* free to talk about Robert Frost and Carl Sandburg as well as Milton and Whittier. Much the same relief was experienced by instructors in other subjects. For many schools it seemed like the opening of a marvelous era.

Nevertheless, the New Plan was far from being universally popular. Clearly, if it was widely adopted, it would mean the death of tutoring or "cramming" schools. It brought dismay to teachers who had specialized in preparing candidates for the old type of examinations. One Latin teacher, who had been drilling boys for thirty years in the same textbook, threw up his hands when he heard that the new examination would be largely at sight and exclaimed, "But how am I going to know what passage they will choose?" To this doctrine, Professor Corwin replied:

Rigidity of requirements with respect to subjects of study, —and this applies even to Latin,—may divert attention from the more essential requisites,—scholastic achievement, native ability, proven industry and interest, and aptitude for advanced work. If the student has these, all else will be added unto him.

Strictly speaking, the Board was neutral on these and other modern movements in education. Discussing in 1923 its attitude towards innovations, the Secretary said:

The College Entrance Examination Board endeavors to maintain an open-minded attitude towards any research relating to the principles which underlie its work and towards any changes that are suggested in its organization. It is the policy of the Board to consider no question as closed and no problem as solved if it is regarded as still unsettled by educators in good standing who have given it careful attention. . . . When one considers the vast influence of the Board in matters educational, one must acknowledge that it is the duty of the Board to refrain from enlisting on either side of a controversial question. It should not proclaim its belief or disbelief in any new doctrine, theory, or procedure until competent investigators possessing the necessary technical equipment have reached conclusions acceptable to the scientific and educational world.

Professor Fiske, as a tactful executive, was carefully endeavoring not to offend any of the Board members or clients. The truth is that the Board simply could not remain static in the midst of mobile ideas. From its inception, it had not shrunk from experimentation, and it had to keep abreast of new movements in its own field. Indeed, it was at times one of the first by whom the new was tried. The history of the first quarter of the present century in American education is necessarily concerned with the philosophy of John Dewey, then beginning to be better understood, and with the lessons learned by educational psychologists from the First World War. From neither of these could the Board have possibly remained aloof.

Offered first in June and September, 1916, the New Plan examinations were taken by only 495 candidates in 1916, 580 in 1917, and 752 in 1918. In 1923 the Secretary reported that during the four-year period from 1920 to 1923 inclusive the Board examinations were taken by 70,633 candidates of whom only 10,419 presented themselves under the New Plan. After it had been in operation for eight years, seven colleges—Smith, Wellesley, Harvard, Vassar, Yale, Mount Holyoke, and Princeton, named in the order of the number of candidates from each—were responsible for most of these taking the comprehensive examinations.

At this period, it must be remembered, the Board consisted largely of representatives of the Eastern colleges. The Middle West and its great state universities were indifferent to the Board and its work, and the Far West and Deep South, still committed to admission by certificate, ignored it. By the 1920's, as we have seen, the strong women's colleges were taking a very active part in its deliberations; while Harvard, Yale, and Princeton, having sponsored the New Plan, were eager to make it succeed. Numerous graduates of Western secondary schools were, of course, obliged to take the Board examinations if they wished to qualify for Eastern colleges, and their teachers had naturally to familiarize themselves with Board policies. While considerations of time and money prevented the Board from appointing any large proportion of Examiners or Readers from too great a distance, an attempt was made to make the groups as national as possible. But the Board, although it hardly deserved to be called sectional, was still largely an Eastern institution.

Even outsiders, however, had developed a wholesome respect for the standards which the Board conscientiously upheld. It was continuing each year to bring together college and secondary teachers for the interchange of professional ideas. No one of the Board's many commissions completed its assignment without adding to the store of educational knowledge. Friendships were easily formed and gladly fostered. Even "crack-pots" and "die-hards," sitting around a table together, learned not to underestimate one another. Many a teacher who, confined to his own campus, had waxed sarcastic over the innovations of the Board, found himself, after working with his fellow-craftsmen at other schools, far more tolerant of its policies. All this brought about a harmony of purpose, a unity of aim, which would not have been possible in 1900.

Out of the many projects sponsored by the Board during this lively post-war period, two or three may be chosen as indicating the general trend. In 1915 the Committee of Review received authorization to organize a new Commission for making a careful study of the requirements in Latin. The chairman was Professor Clifford H. Moore, of Harvard, a scholar who had had some experience in preparatory school teaching, and on it were several men of distinguished reputation, such as Professor Clarence M. Mendell, of Yale, John C. Kirtland, of the Phillips Exeter Academy, and Professor W. W. Wetmore, of Williams—eleven members in all, five from secondary schools and six from colleges. This Commission strongly recommended periodic changes in the Latin texts prescribed for intensive study, but it appeared at the meeting of the Board held in November, 1919, that a protest had arisen against any alteration in the requirements. The Committee of Review, trusting in the democratic process, circularized a large number of educational institutions, with the result that the colleges voted, 12 to 5, and the schools, 22 to 4, in favor of a reduction in the amount of prescribed text to be read as a basis for the more detailed examination questions. Here, again, the fundamental issue was flexibility versus rigidity, and the Board's long campaign of education was showing results. When the Report of the Committee of Review was accepted by the Board without any vigorous dissent, the traditional pedagogy of many decades suffered a body-blow.

The subject of History presented quite a different problem—that of reconciling the various courses and methods of instruction which had grown up since it became a keystone of the curriculum. Latin had long been standardized; History was so young in the schools that it had no generally recognized norm. In April, 1921, the Committee of Review appointed a Commission to revise the definition of the history requirements with a view to its "radical simplification." Again a man of national reputation was named as chairman—Professor David S. Muzzey, of Columbia—and with him ten other members, including Philip P. Chase, of Harvard, Archibald Freeman, of Andover, and Professor S. K. Mitchell, of Yale. This Commission spent two years preparing the report which was approved by the Board in April, 1923. The new definition fixed clearer and narrower limits for the several historical fields and suggested only four examinations—Ancient History, European History, English History, and American History —to replace the eight previously offered. A table prepared in 1919 showing the percentage of books rated 60 or higher in each subject revealed History as standing by far the lowest, with only 35.9 percent, as compared with 45.2 percent in English, 51.1 percent in Mathematics, and 66 percent in Greek. Clearly the preparation of candidates in History still left much to be desired; here, again, the enterprise of the Commission helped to achieve a badly needed reform.

By 1925 the collection of documents published by the Board had become most impressive. Document 117, appearing on December 1, 1925, as the quarter-century ended, gave the requirements for 1926, including lists of experiments in the natural sciences, a description of the comprehensive examinations, and a definition of the unit of admission requirements. In addition to the formidable array of published material, the Board had sent out each year under Professor Fiske's editorship booklets containing copies of the examination papers in each subject, together with enough miscellaneous bulletins to crowd several shelves. The Secretary never lost his passion for statistical tables, which he kindly interpreted for the benefit of his less mathematically-minded associates.

At the annual meeting in November, 1916, Dean Hurlbut, who was being overwhelmed by administrative duties of many varieties, resigned as the Board's chairman and was replaced by Professor Corwin, whose competence for the position was everywhere recognized. After carrying on through the difficult war period, he retired in 1919 as chairman, to be followed by Howard McClenahan, Dean of Princeton. Suave and adroit in dealing with persons and crises, McClenahan was a hard fighter, giving and taking no quarter, but cherishing no grudges when the clash was over. Behind a somewhat formal manner was a highly emotional nature which made him at times a storm center on his campus. His colleagues regarded him as exceptionally able, and he was at least once a leading, although unsuccessful, candidate for the presidency of Princeton. It was, perhaps, his weakness that he enjoyed being the "Boss" and did not willingly delegate authority, but he never shirked an obligation. He was the first chairman to take an active and curious interest in the details of office operation and attempted to formulate rules for Dr. Fiske's guidance. He was a stanch advocate of the New Plan, stressing its virtues at every opportunity.

Mary Emma Woolley, elected to the presidency of Mount Holyoke College in 1900, at the age of thirty-eight, was for thirty-four years its willing and capable delegate to the Board meetings. Her election as Chairman in 1923 was not only an appropriate recognition of the support which the women's colleges had given to the Board but also a tribute to her personality and qualities of leadership. She was a gracious woman, but her strong will was apparent beneath her affability, and in discussion she never expected any special consideration because of her sex. In her conduct of meetings, like all the other women chairmen, she was rather formal and attentive to protocol. She had her foibles, well known to those close to her, and some of her opinions aroused antagonism; but she must be rated, as Dr. Ferry has said, "as one of the most effective of college Presidents and most outstanding of New England women."

Among those increasingly influential in the Board's councils after the First World War was Henry Pennypacker, who, after a decade (1910–20) as Headmaster of the Boston Latin School, became the chairman of the Harvard Committee on Admissions. He was a rugged man, physically, intellectually, and spiritually, with a sonorous voice and impressive bearing which might have made him a distinguished actor or preacher. His eyes and smile were so kindly that cynics wondered how he could say "No"; but he was not soft in his job. He always kept a chess board on his office table, and after an exasperating interview he would turn to it and try to solve some complicated problem against an opponent who could not talk back. Like Dean McClenahan, he was an enthusiast for the New Plan, and he was largely responsible for its rapid spread, especially at Harvard.

Adam Leroy Jones, a Williams graduate in the class of 1895, was associated with Columbia during most of his life, in the Department of Philosophy. In 1909, rather against his inclination, he was appointed Director of University Admissions at Columbia and in that capacity was soon closely identified with the Board, becoming a member in 1917. Modest, tactful, and clearheaded, he was a first-rate committee worker, always accepting more than his share of routine labor. Although connected with the Board for a shorter period than some of the others, he made himself felt decisively on important issues. Only his sudden and premature death kept him from becoming its chairman.

The most provocative member of the Board in his prime was undoubtedly William Allan Neilson. Scottish by birth and training, he held professorships in English at Bryn Mawr, Columbia, and Harvard, but finally in 1917 became President of Smith College and from then until his death in 1946 was associated with the College Entrance Examination Board. Even after he had retired from Smith in 1939, the Board elected him an honorary member-at-large, as they had done for Butler, Farrand, and others. His younger admirers cannot forget how he would sit with his chin held in his nervous fingers, listening to debates with subdued and tolerant mirth in his restless enigmatical eyes. He was one of the most stimulating of talkers, backing his arguments with his profound scholarship, clever analogies, penetrating wit, and keenly observant mind. He once relieved a tense situation by declaring that the best and most rigorously selective plan of admissions was the system in Scotland, where the applicant paid the Registrar a guinea, got his receipt, and was allowed to matriculate. "For," said Neilson, "no Scotchman would pay a guinea for anything he could not use to the fullest!" With his aquiline nose and grizzled Van Dyck beard, he resembled a Renaissance courtier. It was said of him as a teacher that "he made the grim business of learning seem an appealing and blithe adventure"; and Miss Comstock once remarked, "We may think of him as one who demonstrated to an extraordinary degree the virtues of the profession to which as members of this Board we all belong, without succumbing to any of the vices." In Board discussions President Neilson deserved the title which Winston Churchill once bestowed on Harry Hopkins—"Lord Root-of-the Matter."

Dean Heermance has obligingly written down his impressions of the Board as he first knew it.

I wish I could sit with you in the Trustees' Room of the Columbia University Library and reconstruct meetings of the Board in 1922 and thereafter. I have a real nostalgia for that room,—fine polished woodwork, lofty and sufficiently spacious for our fifty or sixty representatives and guests,— the portraits of the good and great added dignity to the comfort of our surroundings, and the heavy carved table in the middle of the room gave the intimate touch of the small conference.

There were only three privileged to sit at that table. The Chairman was at the south end in a chair fit for the Governor of a Province. At his right, always immaculately attired in a most formal cutaway coat, was Dr. Fiske, a handsome man with abundant white hair and strong features. At his right was Miss McLean, his able secretary. The Chairman would, with great courtesy, refer a question to Dr. Fiske, and he with equal courtesy would refer it to Miss McLean, for usually she alone knew the answer.

Behind the Chairman were seated Pennypacker, of Harvard, McClenahan, of Princeton, and Corwin, of Yale. Over to the right were Farrand and Ferry, with Adam Leroy Jones, of Columbia, President Comfort, President Macmillan, and many others. To the left, in a little exclusive group of their own, were the delightful women representatives of the Board to whom the Chairman rightly deferred with great respect, for Miss Pendleton, Miss Woolley, Miss Park, and Dean Gildersleeve clarified many a complicated argument, or at least pacified by their charm irate speakers. Farther to the left and near the table usually sat a gentleman, attentive, tolerant, somewhat amused and ready on the instant to go to the heart of any question,—President Neilson.

In the days of twenty-five years ago the ones who took the most active part in the affairs of the Board were Corwin, McClenahan, and Pennypacker, with Farrand, Ferry, and Fiske the three veterans who knew the struggles and problems of the early days of the organization.

How much had the Board actually grown during a quarter of a century? In 1925 its examinations were attended by 19,775 candidates at 316 centers scattered throughout the world; 1,691 secondary schools—855 public and 836 private—supplied the boys and girls who took the tests. The number of Readers that year in all subjects had reached the astounding total of 626, of whom 146 were for English alone, and 115 for Latin. They came from 200 colleges and universities, 123 public schools, and 303 private schools. It had literally become necessary to "hire a hall" in order to make them all comfortable. Through the Examiners and Readers the methods and decisions of the Board were interpreted to the teaching profession. No other organization of educators could possibly have functioned year after year, with new members coming and old ones going, but always with a restraining nucleus to keep it from running wild or upsetting the apple cart. The expenditures of the Board per candidate had increased from $6.89 in 1919 to $9.32 in 1925. The receipts from all sources in 1925 had been $203,965.92 against expenses of $186,-707.21, and the Custodians at last had money in the bank to invest. With financial security and the confidence of its patrons, the Board was fulfilling the hopes of its founders.

All this good news was stressed faithfully and exultantly by Secretary Fiske in the 25th *Annual Report*.

For a quarter of a century the Board has impressed its influence upon the educational community in many ways. It has issued nearly two hundred thousand certificates reporting upon approximately nine hundred thousand separate examinations. It has dealt with one hundred fifty thousand different candidates, five thousand secondary schools, and five hundred colleges. From a small beginning it has won general recognition as the most potent influence in America for sound standards in secondary education.

Further to substantiate his claim, Professor Fiske added that during the quarter century approximately 450 men and women had served as Examiners and 1,500 as Readers—among them "many who have achieved eminence as successful teachers, many who are distinguished for their learning, and many from whom have come literary and scientific works of permanent value."

At the April meeting in 1925 the Executive Committee announced the appointment of a Committee of Arrangements to make such plans as might seem desirable for the observance of the Board's twenty-fifth birthday. Very appropriately, Miss Woolley was appointed chairman, with Professor Corwin, Dr. Farrand, President Ferry, Dr. Clyde Furst, and President Pendleton as her associates. An Honorary Committee of One Thousand was named, consisting of prominent educators throughout the country who were willing to sponsor the work of the Board. On this committee the two leading figures were, of course, ex-President Eliot and President Butler; but it also included many younger persons who had recently joined the Board—Radcliffe Heermance, director of admissions at Princeton, Carl C. Brigham, associate professor of Psychology at Princeton, Richard M. Gummere, then headmaster of the William Penn Charter School, E. Gordon Bill, dean of Dartmouth College, and others who will be heard from later in this history.

As a preliminary to the main event, nearly 700 Examiners and Readers assembled on June 22, 1925, in the Barnard College Gymnasium and there presented to Professor Fiske a purse of gold and a silver bowl inscribed as follows:

Presented to Thomas Scott Fiske by the Examiners and Readers of the College Entrance Examination Board as a token of regard and high appreciation of the contribution which as Secretary for twenty-four years he has made to the cause of education.

The presentation was made by Professor Nelson Glenn McCrea, who had been Senior Chief Reader of the Latin papers ever since the Board was organized. On the same occasion Dr. Farrand delivered a brief historical survey of the Board's origins and evolution.

The anniversary dinner, held on the evening of Friday, November 6, at the Park Lane Hotel, with more than three hundred college and school representatives present, was the most ambitious social event yet undertaken by the Board. Dr. Eliot was unable to be present, but sent a short letter from his summer home at Northeast Harbor, Maine, concluding with the sentence, "The Board seems to me to have been well conceived and managed and to have made itself useful." He died within a year.

In his typical example of understatement, Dr. Eliot cautiously avoided extravagance or self-laudation. The speakers at the dinner, however, were more effusive, and praise was distributed with discriminating lavishness. Miss Woolley presided and spoke briefly. The others on the program were Henry S. Pritchett, president of the Carnegie Foundation; Dr. Julius Sachs; President Ellen F. Pendleton; Dr. Farrand; and by logical inevitability, President Butler. On the following morning at the regular session of the Board, resolutions were adopted congratulating President Butler, thanking the trustees of Columbia University and Barnard College for their many courtesies and kindnesses, thanking the president, director, and faculty of the Union Theological Seminary for providing quarters and facilities when they were badly needed, expressing the appreciation of the Board "to such examiners, readers, and supervisors as have served the Board for over twenty years and to such others as the Chairman and the Secretary may find worthy of such expression"—and finally praising Secretary Fiske "as an executive combining a genius for detail and a rare gift of broad vision." It would seem that everybody went away happy.

Early in 1926 a volume entitled *The Work of the Col-*

lege Entrance Examination Board, 1901–1925 was edited and published by Professor Fiske. It contained the addresses at the anniversary dinner, together with the historical paper by Dr. Farrand, an article by President Lowell, of Harvard, and a digest of the publications of the Board. To the historian for the fiftieth anniversary this volume has been indispensable.

Although it was not apparent in 1925, the Board was closing one stage of its evolution and about to move fearlessly into another. The setting off of its first quarter century as a period by itself is not merely chronological or artificial. It happened that a new era was dawning in the development of educational theory—perhaps not any better, but certainly different. Soon the Board was to become a leader in a movement which is still going on today and which, for good or ill, is likely to continue for some time.

CHAPTER V

APTITUDE
TESTS

The Board's experiments with comprehensive examinations had demonstrated that it was alert, not averse to change and willing "to be shown." Now in the stimulating postwar era of the 1920's it threw out a challenge to all American education. In its research on what were first called "intelligence tests," it began by following a partly blazed trail, but later took the lead and did its own pioneering. Neither timid on the one hand nor fanatical on the other, it chose rather to pursue without prejudice and in a relentless scientific spirit what seemed to be the truth. Of all its services, this was probably the most sensational and seems likely to be the most lasting. The contrast between the examinations offered by the individual colleges in 1899 and those sponsored by the Board forty years later is nothing short of startling; a pedagogical Rip Van Winkle who went to sleep in 1920 and returned to consciousness in 1940 would have been indeed bewildered. Throughout the movement towards the improvement of "intelligence tests" the College Entrance Examination Board appeared to be waving banners in a crusade and was praised or damned depending on the philosophy of the observer; but whatever else may be said of it during this phase of

its history, it was never guilty of claiming too much.
Nor did it act as a drag on the chariot of progress, although impatient psychologists even made this accusa-
tion. It displayed a proper balance between enthusiasm
and caution. This proves that it was wisely advised and
led.

The first intimation in the official reports that anything was stirring came in 1919, when Dr. Fiske, writing
under the heading "Comprehensive Examinations as
Intelligence Tests," remarked:

It should be the purpose of the College Entrance Examination Board not only to ascertain whether the candidates
have acquired the information and methods of thought
necessary for successful work in college, but also to determine whether they possess certain important intellectual
qualities which are sometimes described as alertness, power,
and endurance, although these terms would seem to indicate excellencies of the body rather than of the mind.
Up to the present time the Board's endeavors in this direction are exhibited most conspicuously in the comprehensive
examinations. If these examinations continue to respond to
the demands of the times they should eventually become
the best possible tests combining the necessary elements of
an informational and of a mental, or psychological, character.

In November, 1920, "because of the growing interest
in general intelligence examinations and other new
types of examinations," the Board, following a procedure which had now become routine, appointed a commission, with Headmaster W. R. Marsh, of St. Paul's
School, Garden City, Long Island, as chairman, and
including Professor Corwin, Professor S. P. Hayes, of

Mount Holyoke College, Professor Adam Leroy Jones, of Columbia, and Stanley R. Yarnall, of Germantown Friends School, near Philadelphia. The members were requested "to investigate and report on general intelligence examinations and other new types of examinations offered in several secondary school subjects."

The First World War brought about an astonishing expansion in the scientific measurement of human intelligence. With millions of young draftees as their victims, the psychologists had a field day. The American Psychological Association and the National Research Council early formed plans which won the approval of the military authorities and were later carried out by the Committee for Classification of Personnel in the Army—the CCPA—particularly in the famous Army Alpha and Army Beta tests, which made it possible to sort out soldiers in a rough way according to their abilities and potentialities. The experts knew very well that these tests were not infallible; but they did at least enable post commanders to distinguish quickly between morons on the one hand and bright "officer material" on the other. Before hostilities ceased, these tests had been widely used in army camps and greatly improved.

After the Armistice, men who had administered these intelligence tests brought them home and talked about them in their own communities, feeling that they might be useful in peacetime. Leading members of the CCPA, Dr. Edward L. Thorndike, Dr. Beardsley Ruml, and Dr. Walter V. Bingham, and its director, Colonel Walter Dill Scott, were regarded as educational missionaries, the spreaders of an important gospel. Professor John J. Coss became so much excited that he wanted to talk about nothing else, and when he resumed his collegiate duties at Columbia he complained: "It's hard to come back to a milk diet after having lived on raw meat!" I can remember returning to my teaching job full of hope, believing that at last we had a means of prediction which, when perfected, would be superior to any previously known type of examination.

Secretary Fiske, an unerring barometer of the sentiment of the Board, wrote in 1924:

The Board wishes to ascertain in regard to the boys and girls entering college not merely whether they have stored in their memories the contents of the textbooks in general use but primarily whether they have made a start, have actually gone a little distance on the road from childhood to intellectual maturity.

The examinations of the Board up to that date, according to Professor Fiske, had been above all a test of the following attributes:

(1) Power of expression
(2) Intelligent appreciation
(3) Ability to reassemble information
(4) Courage to form and express independent judgments
(5) Concentration, or power to sustain a mental effort.

Having made this summary of what had been accomplished, the Secretary turned to a tentative future program:

Among the qualities in regard to which many colleges desire information and for which direct tests exist, although the Board has not as yet undertaken to administer such tests, are the following,—

(1) Ethical behavior

(2) Physical health

(3) Powers of observation

(4) Mental alertness

(5) Ability to participate successfully in cooperative efforts or team work

(6) Skill in laboratory work

(7) Facility in conversation in foreign languages.

Obviously a good deal of fireside and across-the-table discussion was going on during this period between optimists and skeptics, conservatives and liberals. Mr. Marsh's commission, appointed in 1920, was in no haste to make recommendations and seemingly indulged in deliberate delay; but in 1922 the full Board adopted innocuous resolutions declaring that it looked "with favorable interest" on the use of "general intelligence examinations" and stood ready to co-operate in giving them just as soon as that was practicable. The Chairman was then authorized to appoint still another commission "to consider the question of the desire for intelligence examinations and the feasibility of the proposal that the Board participate in their conduct."

At the moment, Chairman Howard McClenahan consulted educational psychologists, who advised him that the time was not ripe, and accordingly he did nothing. In April, 1924, however, the Board reiterated its resolutions of two years before, and Miss Woolley, who had succeeded Dean McClenahan as chairman, appointed a distinguished commission representing the best thought on the Board. Dean E. Gordon Bill, of Dartmouth, was chairman, and associated with him were Dean Joseph S. Ames, of Johns Hopkins, Radcliffe Heermance, of Princeton, Professor G. W. McClelland, of Pennsylvania, President William A. Neilson, of Smith, President Ellen F. Pendleton, of Wellesley, and Dean.C. Mildred Thompson, of Vassar. No one of them could have qualified as an expert in the relatively new field of psychological testing, but they were all persons of experience on the college level, not easily swayed by pressure groups and addicted to cool-headed scrutiny of innovations.

The Commission held several exciting meetings, examined the evidence, and presented their conclusions at the meeting of the Board in the following November. Leaving deliberately aside the question of the value of "psychological tests," they reported that many colleges were already using them and accordingly recommended that the Board enter into an agreement with the National Research Council or some other qualified agency through which such tests could be prepared for its patrons—just as, under similar circumstances, the Board had embarked on the adventure of the "New Plan." After some amusing discussion, the Board approved the recommendation of the Commission and appointed an Advisory Committee of experts to formulate a procedure "for the preparation of psychological tests." This included three men—Professor Carl C. Brigham, of Princeton, as chairman, Professor Henry T. Moore, of Dartmouth, and Professor Robert M. Yerkes, of Yale. They were all at the top of their profession, but it was not long before Professor Brigham, with his intellectual stability and tremendous driving power, was by common consent made the spokesman of the Board whenever decisions had to be reached.

One cannot escape the conclusion that the Board,

without fully realizing what had happened, soon found itself in deeper water than some of the members liked. Certain New England headmasters distrusted the whole idea and resorted to ridicule instead of argument in a campaign to make the new tests unpopular. There was plenty of good-natured banter at the annual meetings of the Headmasters' Association, with scornful references to "raw scores," "bogie-grades," "coefficients of correlation," "tetrads," and "sigmas," and many a funny anecdote was based on the esoteric jargon of experts. It was altogether too easy to be humorous at the expense of some of the "crack-pots" who were voicing extravagant claims. But Professor Brigham's quiet tones and dignified manner were disconcerting to opponents who wanted him to fight back. He never made the mistake of overstating his case; indeed he was the first to admit that not too much could or should be expected from "psychological tests" as they were then available. His very caution made more converts than he could have won by pounding the table. What resulted from all the palaver was a very healthful clarification of the issues. President Neilson, for example, was skeptical of the plan as it was at first proposed; yet even he was persuaded by the steady accumulation of favorable testimony.

In April, 1925, the Board accepted the recommendation of the Committee of Review that "psychological tests" be administered in June and September, 1926. The commission appointed to prepare and score the tests inevitably included Professor Brigham, as chairman, and with him were Professor Angier, of Yale, Professor MacPhail, of Brown, Professor Rogers, of Smith, and Professor Stone, of Dartmouth. No secondary school representative was identified with the plan in its earlier stages, probably because nobody on that level could qualify as an authority. The Board had now reached a new stage in its evolution, one which could never have been prognosticated by its founders. But even conservative educators, as the twentieth century swept along, were becoming reconciled to rapid and comprehensive changes.

Setting promptly to work, the Brigham Committee —as it came to be called—produced within a short period a manual on what they chose to style the "Scholastic Aptitude Test." They selected this title in the belief that the adjective "psychological" in that connection was inaccurate and misleading. In their preface they very wisely introduced a paragraph of warning.

The present state of all efforts of men to measure or in any way estimate the worth of other men, or to evaluate the results of their nurture, or to reckon their potential possibilities does not warrant any certainty of prediction. . . . This additional test now made available through the instrumentality of the College Entrance Examination Board may help to resolve a few perplexing problems, but it should be regarded merely as a supplementary record. To place too great emphasis on test scores is as dangerous as the failure properly to evaluate any score or rank in conjunction with other measures and estimates which it supplements.

The chief danger came from thoughtless "all-outers," who, in spite of warnings, treated the new tests as an infallible means of predicting future success. Already in school faculty meetings instructors were speaking of a student's "I.Q." as if it were a permanent label. Fortunately the Board itself was guarded by Brigham's conservative counsel against the perils of overenthusiasm. He was like the research worker in cancer who hesitates even to mention a cure, fearing that victims of the disease may expect too much.

A human dynamo, Brigham wore himself out at an age when he should have been in his golden prime. His activity throughout this period was inspiring to those around him, and he once declared that he had toiled eighteen years without a vacation. In one conference after another he sought for questions which could be used on the test papers. He tried simultaneously to remedy imperfections, to reduce the percentage of error, to correct wrong impressions, to eliminate prejudice, and to restrain impetuosity. That the Scholastic Aptitude Test won so quickly the confidence of the educational world is due mainly to Brigham's patience and dogged perseverance.

After all these preliminaries, the first Board Scholastic Aptitude Test was administered on June 23, 1926, to 8,040 candidates, of whom 1,257 were applying for Yale, 1,176 for Pennsylvania, 918 for Princeton, 865 for Smith, 742 for Wellesley, 602 for Vassar, and 536 for Harvard, the others being scattered over a wide area. Practice booklets containing samples of all the various tests had been sent out to candidates one week before the examination, so that they might know what to expect. The scoring was carried out by clerks recruited from the undergraduate bodies of Princeton and Columbia, working under the supervision of a staff composed of instructors and graduate students in psychology. Some irregularities inevitably occurred, and in spite of every precaution accidents happened; but for the most part things went well. In commenting on this first trial, the Committee said:

The general plan of testing employed in this work follows conventional procedures rather closely. . . . It does not seem unreasonable to expect improvement in both the validity and reliability of the tests as time goes on. The committee, at the start, finds no problem involved that does not show promise of a satisfactory empirical solution.

Secretary Fiske, in his *Report* for 1927, emphasized the Board's "careful investigation upon a scale hitherto unprecedented into the significance and value of psychological examinations" and added that it was thus making "a permanent contribution of the highest importance to educational progress." Year after year Professor Brigham made his own comments, in language sometimes packed with technical jargon rather puzzling for the lay reader, but always presenting the conclusions with honesty even when the experiments were less successful than had been hoped. During the first two trial years the program was composed of nine subtests, as follows: Definitions, Arithmetical Problems, Classification, Artificial Language, Antonyms, Number Series, Analogies, Logical Inference, and Paragraph Reading. In 1928 these were reduced to seven, and in 1929 to six. In 1929, after very careful observation, Professor Brigham stated that it had become necessary to divide the Scholastic Aptitude Test into two distinct parts— one to determine literary or linguistic ability, the other mathematical or scientific fitness. His comment on this decision is also an indication of the quality of his mind.

The committee must now consider the possibility of adding a mathematical aptitude section to the present scholastic aptitude test to make the test more generally useful for engineering colleges or for the selection of scientific students in colleges of the more general type. The present scholastic aptitude test seems quite definitely related to English, Latin, History, and the more general reading courses in college. It may be pictured as measuring the varying degrees of literacy to be found in college applicant populations. It is limited in scope in that it seems to deal only with verbal symbolism, a type of symbolic thinking which is of prime importance if the student is expected to derive benefit from lectures and textbooks, but which is not of paramount importance in mathematics and science. A supplementary test of thinking in mathematical symbolism might serve the double function of revealing students who might profitably continue in the scientific fields, and of exposing those students whose proposed election of a scientific curriculum is the result of a verbal disability rather than a high degree of mathematical and scientific aptitude.

By April, 1930, Professor Brigham's services had become so indispensable that the Executive Committee recommended his appointment as Associate Secretary. It was understood that he would remain in full standing on the Princeton faculty as Professor of Psychology and retain his Chairmanship of the Commission on Scholastic Aptitude Tests. The Board had by this date opened its own laboratory in Princeton, which Brigham and his assistants were using as an experiment station. The appointment of Brigham as a salaried member of the Board staff was a recognition of the fact that his contribution had made an impression on college admissions officers.

The Commission on Scholastic Aptitude Tests had been puzzled by what it described as "the persistence of individual idiosyncrasy"—a phenomenon fairly familiar to preparatory school headmasters. The differences between the scores on the verbal and the mathematical portions of the tests were so striking as to attract the attention of the Examiners, who pondered long over the problem without reaching any satisfactory explanation. In 1932 Professor Brigham published a little volume entitled *A Study of Error,* in which he considered more than a thousand test items or questions, analyzing their usefulness. He was constantly on the watch to check the results from the employment of questions of a certain type or trend. His educational philosophy was never static from one season to another.

The restlessness of the years following 1929—the period of widespread economic depression—showed itself in criticisms, covert and open, of the College Entrance Examination Board and its new policies. Secretary Fiske noted in 1933 that there had been many attacks on the Board, particularly because of its alleged harmful influence upon the activities of the secondary schools. The Executive Committee, meanwhile, had recognized another source of hostile comment by asking Professor Brigham to recommend "ways and means by which the examinations of the Board may be given greater prognostic value, especially in the upper ranges."

In his thoughtful answer to this request, Professor

Brigham, referring to the "present feeling of uneasiness on the part of the Board," spoke of its "essentially dualistic nature" as being largely responsible. By way of explanation, he continued:

The conflicting motives would be most easily brought to light by asking the Board to decide whether its examinations should measure *institutions* or *individuals*. The Board's present high position in the educational world is the direct result of its efficacy as a form of *institutional* control. Its chief weakness lies in its somewhat inadequate descriptions of individuals seeking admission to college.

Following this preface, Professor Brigham, in a timely and dispassionate discussion of conflicting theories, commented on the desire of the Progressive Education Association to have a limited number of high-stand candidates exempted from all examinations by the colleges and also devoted some attention to the so-called "new type" movement for objective tests. He pointed out that the Board had thus far developed into an organization of *Readers* rather than of *Examiners* and that during the preceding twelve years it had spent more than a million dollars for reading and less than forty-three thousand dollars for examining. In conclusion, he advised that the Board, as a responsible examining body, should take steps leading to the improvement of its measuring devices, adding that the Board would make a great advance if it assumed a research function and deliberately attacked its problems experimentally. What he wanted, he confessed, was "the virility of a frankly experimental attack."

All the vague dissatisfaction and accompanying clash

of opinion were evidence of a lack of common agreement on the aims and methods of examining. A multiplicity of words was used in addresses at educational associations by teachers who wanted to have their say. The problem which had seemed so simple to President Butler in 1900 had become much more complicated as the psychologists moved into control. They saw in the Board a promising instrument for good. They saw it also undertaking a task which, like that of Sisyphus, could never be completed. It must act as the integrating mechanism between school and college, prepared to change as new ideas became popular.

Not everybody on the Board was convinced that Brigham was on the right track. A few minds as truly liberal as his felt that the Board through his influence was being almost submerged with statistical tables and mathematical terminology and that the human element was being neglected in favor of a cold objectivity. But those who opposed him had themselves no solution to suggest except inertia, and their attitude, consequently, was not constructive. The Board continued, therefore, to accept Professor Brigham as its policy maker, and whatever route was taken for the next few years was charted by him.

In April, 1933, as a means of crystallizing some of the ideas then current, the Executive Committee authorized the appointment of a Sub-Committee on Questions of Policy, to consider the Board's relations to the schools, its general problem of examining, and the probable lines of its future development. Its chairman was Professor Adam Leroy Jones, of Columbia—a quiet, unassuming man who was universally respected and trusted. Associated with him were three other college representatives—Professor C. F. Tucker Brooke, of Yale, Dean Francis L. Knapp, of Wellesley, and Professor Edwin B. Wilson, of Harvard—together with the heads of four secondary schools—Milton Academy, Phillips Academy, Baldwin School, and Malden High School. To the work of this subcommittee Professor Jones gave his best thought. Unfortunately he died on March 2, 1934, shortly after the presentation of his *Report,* but the subcommittee and the Board had already profited by his long experience.

Secretary Fiske described the recommendations of this committee as marking an epoch in the evolution of the Board. Actually they did not involve any sensational changes in operation, but rather the continued and logical development of former policies. Professor Jones was not the man needlessly to defy tradition or to maintain, in free verse or otherwise, that the past was "a bucket of ashes, a sun gone down in the west." He and the other members of the committee could not be unmindful, as he suggested at their first session, that it would be foolish to throw everything overboard because a few joints in the old ship had sprung a leak. In their preamble, the committee said:

Interesting and very promising experiments are in progress in secondary education to-day involving new methods of approach to the whole curriculum, a changing emphasis in fields of study, and new organization of work in many subjects, especially in the social studies and natural science. The Board should be ready to cooperate with the secondary schools and the colleges in this period of important changes in secondary school work.

During its deliberations this committee frequently called upon Professor Brigham for his advice, and they were much influenced by it. Partly because of it, some "old-fashioned" conceptions of examinations were quickly discarded. Understanding that its task was chiefly that of formulating suggestions for the expansion of the Board's current practice, the committee offered specific recommendations. First of all, in order to allow the secondary schools the greater freedom which many of them desired, it indicated its viewpoint, as follows: "That the existing definitions of the requirements be liberally interpreted as indicating in a general way the nature and extent of preparation considered necessary and not as prescribing any definite form of instruction, method of preparation, or teaching technique."

As one symbol of its belief the committee suggested, and the full Board approved, the discontinuance after 1934 of the restricted examination in English, commonly called English 1–2. In the light of recent events this examination had become almost anachronistic, a survival of days when pupils were being trained to remember rather than to think. To some members of the committee who had been teachers of English it seemed as if a great burden had been removed.

In the second place, the committee took up the controversial matter of examinations. It could not fail to perceive that some Examiners, with the purest of motives, had exercised a "police function" in using outworn definitions of requirements as instruments of institutional control. Furthermore separate committees of Examiners had insisted on working out their own techniques, which had often been at variance with the modern philosophy of the Board. Hence the committee, frequently employing Professor Brigham's own phraseology, recommended that the Committee of Revision be reconstituted and given broad authority "to supervise, review, and coordinate the examination policies of the Board" and that its functions include "the analyzing subject by subject of the Board examinations in order to discover new methods of increasing their validity and reliability." Obviously the Committee on Questions of Policy were aiming to emphasize the research aspect of the Board, to encourage experimentation, and to produce a higher degree of consistency in operation.

In the third place, the committee dealt briefly with the recurring problem of the fluctuation of marks from year to year. Some of the discrepancies had been almost scandalous, as, for example, when the Physics paper for 1926 "passed" 52.8 percent, while two years later the proportion rose to 81.9 percent. The *Report* of the committee made an appropriate and sensible comment: "In the face of such eccentric results it seems more conservative to assume that the populations are comparatively stable and that the examinations vary in difficulty than to assume that the examinations are constant and that the selection of pupils and the quality of the preparations vary."

To avoid these difficulties the committee recommended a process of "rescaling," by which the grade of 60 would be so fixed that approximately 65 percent of the candidates would fall at or above this point and 35 percent below it. The Board gave this proposal implementation by voting to rescale marks in all subjects so that the grades year in and year out would be more consistent. The Old Guard in the Headmasters' Association, led by Horace D. Taft, waged unceasing war on this policy as artificial and thoroughly unsound and indulged in many "wise-cracks" at the expense of the Board.

In the fourth place, the committee, again in a thoroughly progressive spirit, took steps to eradicate what they believed to be the obsolescent notion of the hard and fast unit representing exposure to a course lasting for one hundred and twenty sixty-minute hours, or their equivalent, and to substitute for it what they described as the conception "of placement on the basis of a measured amount of achievement." The idea was expressed in the recommendation "that the modern language Examiners gradually work away from the two, three, and four-unit concepts and develop placement examinations in the modern foreign languages."

For some years there had been protests against the "highly factual" character of the Board's examinations in History. The more vehement critics maintained that History had degenerated into almost as much a "memory discipline" as Latin had been in the 1880's, and insisted that too little stress was laid on developing in students the ability to assemble and relate materials and weigh evidence. To satisfy both conservatives and progressives, the committee recommended the appointment of a commission "to study the possibility of a comprehensive examination in History based upon a continuous four-year course and to consider the advisability of setting in each branch of History an examination partly of objective questions and partly of essay-type questions." The issue, as it soon appeared, was highly controversial, and the mere intimation of any such "reform" in some quarters almost turned brother against brother. Charges of bad faith and "educational sabotage" were so frequent as to cause alarm; but the committee had no intention of yielding ground, even under sharp fire. They had evolved their pattern and intended to cut their cloth accordingly. Any other policy would have been shamefully inconsistent—and cowardly.

Finally the committee adopted *in toto* Professor Brigham's conception of an "integrated course" in science as opposed to "the memorization of facts under separate rubrics." To further this very modern doctrine, it recommended the appointment of still another commission, "to study the possibility of a comprehensive examination based upon a continuous four-year course in science," and suggested that it provide, as an alternative to the usual examination in Physics, a three-hour examination devised to test the extent to which the student had brought to the enrichment of a study of Physics the facts and principles learned in earlier studies of Biology, Chemistry, or Astronomy.

The somewhat startling proposals of the committee went through the customary routine of approval by the Executive Committee and the Committee of Review, and were then adopted at the meeting of the Board on November 1, 1934, without a dissenting voice. The unanimity was more apparent than real, for there was an undercurrent of opposition quite evident in the low murmurs of those who did not care to expose themselves to the perils of argument. Actually, despite the committee's insistence that it was merely codifying policies already in operation, it was by implication condemning practices to which many excellent teachers were devoted; and resistance quickly revealed itself as soon as the delegates had gone home to think matters over. The committee, guided by Professor Brigham, had had the daring to put together the components of a complete educational philosophy, and for this reason its contribution was important. But its conclusions were to be modified, even discarded, before many years had passed.

CHAPTER VI

PROBLEMS

AND

PERSONALITIES

In 1945 John N. Stalnaker, Associate Secretary of the College Entrance Examination Board, said in his final report: "Nine years ago the general outlook for the Board was not bright. There was adverse criticism on every side. The number of candidates under examination had been decreasing for several years."

This statement, if it is not to be misunderstood, requires some clarifying and amplification. The 1930's in the United States constituted an era of "recession," or "depression," and therefore of disturbance and uncertainty. The Board, supported as it was by many of the country's strongest colleges, was never on the verge of collapse; but like banks and factories it found it advisable to take stock and see what could be done to attract more customers. In June, 1926, the examinations were attended by 22,089 boys and girls, 2,314 more than in the previous year. Small increases in numbers were reported annually until 1931, when there was a slight falling off. In 1932, however, the candidates dropped sharply to 19,929, the smallest registration for a long period; and in 1933, when the Democrats came into national power, the situation seemed even more ominous, for the figure announced was only 17,695. In 1934 the total sank to 16,360, and the Board executives began to wonder what was happening; in 1935, when only 15,394 took the tests, it looked to the pessimists as if the Board were heading towards catastrophe. By this date it had already taken precautionary steps, but it was not until 1937 that the downward movement was checked, and then, according to the Secretary, only because of a larger number of girls from both public and private schools. In 1938, to everybody's relief, the Secretary announced that the net registration for the April and June series of examinations was 17,-677, an increase of more than 11 percent over the 1937 series. From that date until the outbreak of the Second World War there was no further cause for alarm.

The reasons for the slump in registration during the 1930's were at the moment not altogether clear, but the financial stringency had affected many families who under normal conditions would have sent their children to college. Furthermore, the progressive schools had persuaded several colleges to allow them to present their best-equipped candidates without examination. Professor Fiske disliked this trend, and in his *Report* for 1932, did not hesitate to say so.

Some of those interested in the work of the College Entrance Examination Board are disturbed by the fact that a number of educational institutions are considering the possibility of admitting without examination students who at the end of their high school course stand in the upper tenth, the upper fifth, or the upper fourth of the class. Some institutions have already adopted this plan, at least tentatively.

It should be unnecessary to argue that educational institutions that admit large numbers of students on the basis of the Board's examinations should refrain from any action likely to make the Board less efficient or to injure its academic standards. If institutions which make use of the Board's examinations should excuse from the examinations the cream of the student body, the Board's Readers would see chiefly the examination papers of second-rate students and would gradually be led to believe that really good examinations are within the power of very few students. The proportion of students failing at the Board's examinations might become so high that the Readers would be under great pressure to give fairly good marks to papers that do not deserve them. Furthermore, to excuse from the Board's examinations a large number of candidates forming a homogeneous group would seriously hinder any statistical study of the results of the examinations.

However right he may have been in principle, the Secretary could not dictate to colleges like Harvard or to the sponsors of the Progressive movement. Furthermore, to fair-minded outsiders the Progressive experiment was well worth watching. But Professor Fiske was not the only one to perceive that if it succeeded completely the usefulness of the Board, at least in its existing form, was likely to be terminated.

Although there had been some justifiable criticism of the Board's examinations, it is not probable that this in itself caused any marked diminution in the number of registrants. Whether they liked the tests or not, applicants for certain colleges had to submit themselves to them, and teachers had to conduct themselves accordingly. The Board itself, while watchful of educational evolution, could not afford to act on impulse and abandon all that had been built up over thirty years. It cannot be maintained, I think, that the Board or its executive officers were afflicted with inertia, obstinacy, or lack of vision. Secretary Fiske had his feelings hurt more than once, but he concealed nothing, conscientiously reported the discontent, and tried to pacify the complainants. As frequently happens in emergencies, two or three imaginative and resolute thinkers, with evidence to back up their theories, gained control and guided the Board out of its Slough of Despond.

Mr. Pennypacker, who succeeded Miss Woolley as Chairman in 1927, held office during a period of relative peace and prosperity. He was followed in 1930 by Miss Ellen F. Pendleton, President of Wellesley College, who had represented that institution on the Board as far back as 1902, when she was Dean, and had continued her active membership after becoming President, in 1911. Very few persons were better acquainted with the Board and its operations, for she had seldom been absent from meetings and had sat on committees which made important decisions. One who knew her well has said, "Miss Woolley seemed to me ultra-feminine, while Miss M. Carey Thomas was ultra-masculine and Miss Pendleton was the perfectly balanced woman." Blessed with a judicial mind, she was instinctively just and impartial and insisted on the full and free expression of opinion. She is still remembered for her "calm, steadfast, friendly, valiant spirit."

Since Dr. Butler's withdrawal it had become the custom for the Chairman to serve not more than three years. Accordingly Miss Pendleton resigned in 1933, and the Board elected in her place Dean Radcliffe

Heermance, of Princeton University. A graduate of Williams College, he had been instructor in English at Lawrenceville and was later associated with Princeton in various capacities, becoming Director of Admissions in 1922. It is far from coincidental that the Board under his chairmanship initiated so many radical and salutary changes in policy. He brought to the position diverse interests, rich experience, emotional maturity, and an understanding of human nature. Fundamentally sympathetic with the views of Professor Brigham, Dean Heermance supported him at crucial moments and worked with him in his attempt to modernize the procedures and techniques of the Board. This general agreement made progress not only possible but also inevitable. A man in whom blood and judgment were well commingled, Heermance could both feel and perceive what ought to be done. In Executive Committee and on the floor of the full Board meeting, after conflicting speakers had left the issue in doubt, he again and again clarified the arguments and pointed the way to a decision. It was he who once, in righteous indignation, rose and said, "This request is unethical. Indeed it is worse than that,—it is a violation of good taste!" More than once, by sheer weight of logic, Dean Heermance has made converts of those who had originally opposed him—an unusual accomplishment.

The shift in direction was further symbolized by the retirement on October 28, 1936, of Professor Fiske as Executive Secretary and Treasurer, after thirty-five years of devoted service. A master of the history of the organization, he sometimes in his later years bored the younger members by dwelling on the past rather than on the future, but nevertheless he had played his role well. He had given his best to the Board during its formative period, and it is hard to imagine how it could have developed so successfully without him. Starting with negligible resources, the Board had grown under his direction from a small body examining 973 candidates prepared at 249 schools for admission to 21 colleges to a complicated organism which at its maximum had examined 25,478 candidates prepared at 1,959 schools for admission to 206 colleges. The annual *Report* for 1937, written by his successor, stresses the fact that during his long and uninterrupted service the usefulness of the Board, at least until the 1930's, steadily increased.

The moment had now arrived for the infusion of younger blood. The old order changeth, giving place to new. When Professor Fiske departed, it needed only a suggestion from Chairman Heermance for the Board to turn unanimously to Professor George W. Mullins, like Fiske a member of the Barnard College faculty. A graduate of the University of Arkansas in the Class of 1904, he had taken his Master's degree at Columbia in 1913 and his Doctorate in 1917, after which he joined the staff of Barnard College in the Department of Mathematics. From 1921 to 1929 he had been the Board's Director of Reading. His place was then taken by Professor Harry W. Redding, head of the Department of Mathematics in the Cooper Union Institute of Technology and at one time lecturer in Mathematics at Columbia. In 1933 Redding, because of other obligations, was obliged to discontinue his work for the Board, and Professor Mullins was persuaded to return. Two years later, when it was announced that Professor Fiske's retirement was imminent, Dr. Mullins was elected to succeed him.

As events turned out, there could not have been a wiser choice. Vigilant, thoughtful, and liberal in his philosophy, Professor Mullins was just the man to collaborate with Professor Brigham in the necessary rehabilitation of the Board. He had already participated in its activities as Examiner, Reader, and Director of Reading and had been welcomed at the Board's councils as a valued adviser. With consummate tact, he often interposed a word of caution when the Research Department seemed, in its enthusiasm, to be running a trifle wild. He could achieve his ends quietly, without injuring anybody's feelings. In short, he was a fine executive, who knew when to drive and when to curb.

Professor Mullins took office at a period when, as we have noted, the Board was endeavoring vigorously, even desperately, to adjust itself to changed conditions. Dean Heermance has written, "The Board would have died in its fine, old-fashioned, four poster bed and have been decently interred had not Brigham brought it new life, —and that new life could never have been nourished and brought to fruition had it not been for Mullins." As early as 1930 Secretary Fiske had thought it desirable to explain the method followed in appointing Readers, saying that an attempt was made each year "to represent every important group of institutions or individuals included in the Board's constituency." He added that no one was justified in stating that he held a permanent appointment as Reader. Nevertheless, a feeling was abroad that some of the Readers had continued in that capacity too long—that they were set in their ways and unresponsive to fresh ideas. The Board had also been criticized for not appointing a larger number of Readers from the public secondary schools. Before long the Committee of Revision, having in mind the long-range program of Professor Brigham and his associates, agreed on a series of recommendations for the consideration of the Executive Committee: that no Reader who had served five years or longer be eligible to reappointment until one year had intervened; that no Reader who had served for eight years or more be reappointed for at least two years; that any Reader who had served in all ten years or more should be placed on a reserve list, if necessary, to make room for new appointments; and that an effort should be made in the future to name Readers to an approximate ratio of four for colleges, three for private schools, and two for public schools. The Executive Committee, in April, 1935, adopted these recommendations as a statement of general policy, and the Board took favorable action accordingly.

As a first step towards installing this broad principle of rotation, the Secretary notified nearly fifty Readers who had served continuously for fourteen years or more that they would not be reappointed in 1935. There was the usual mild grumbling, but most of the superannuated veterans took their discharge cheerfully, recognizing that their day was over. The immediate effect was the bringing in of a younger group, who needed considerable orientation. The Committee of Revision had suggested that there should be an annual turnover of about 15 percent, and that the median age should be close to forty. A sufficient nucleus of experienced Readers remained to prevent any sharp lapse in continuity. The new policy had the advantage of bringing into close contact with the Board a larger and larger number of teachers who, after their indoctrination in New York, went back as missionaries to their own localities, spreading its educational gospel.

The Examiners also were subjected to the same principle of rotation; and in 1936 John M. Stalnaker, only thirty-two years old, a graduate of the University of Chicago and a Research Psychologist at that institution, was invited to meet regularly with the several committees of Examiners, in the expectation that through him a more satisfactory co-ordination among them might be established. As he inspired more and more confidence and himself gained assurance, Mr. Stalnaker brought about a greater consistency among the Examiners in various subjects. Even Examiners who were first-rate classroom teachers did not always understand and were consequently out of sympathy with the objectives of what might be called the New Psychology. It was vital for the interests of the Board that they should be fully informed; and the youthful Stalnaker, combining due humility with persuasion and pressure, was able to make converts without being offensively dogmatic. Neither a politician or a "go-getter," he was a fine example of the pure scientist, confident in the power of truth. As a professional, he was just as much disturbed when his tests were treated as sacrosanct as when they were unmercifully blasted by the ignorant.

Some illustrations will show what was happening

during this transition period to the "old-fashioned" examinations. For English it will be necessary to go back chronologically to 1929, when the Commission on English, headed by Professor Charles Swain Thomas, of Harvard University, a leading authority on the teaching of English in secondary schools, recommended the abolition of the National Conference on Uniform Entrance Requirements in English. In April, 1930, before the full meeting of the Board, Dr. Wilson Farrand gave a delightfully humorous account of the history and accomplishments of this National Conference. One significant paragraph especially deserves quotation because of its reference to current conflicting views.

As time went on the Conference found itself turning more and more toward the comprehensive form of examination, and on one occasion it would probably have substituted the comprehensive examination for the old form if certain of the New England colleges had not protested vigorously and insisted that they must have an examination on certain specific books. As a compromise, therefore, the Conference recommended that two examinations, one restrictive and the other comprehensive, should be set and that the candidate should be given his choice.

In concluding his historical remarks, Dr. Farrand, who had been instrumental in forming the Conference, said: "It has done a great work, but the time has come when this work can be done more efficiently by the College Board, and the Conference, therefore, bows its head meekly to the axe."

As a substitute for the National Conference, the Board appointed a new Commission in English, headed by Professor Harrison R. Steeves, of Columbia, and including, in addition to Dr. Farrand and Dr. Thomas, several other outstanding English teachers in both schools and colleges. Once again the familiar battle between rigidity and flexibility had to be fought out, and once again it resulted in a compromise. The Commission prepared a careful Report, defining certain requirements in English to be effective in June, 1935—a long time ahead—and this was formally approved in 1932. Under the title *Examining the Examination in English,* this report was published by the Harvard University Press and widely distributed. Briefly, it provided for two types of examination—the so-called "Comprehensive" and the "Restricted"—both three hours long —and allowed the candidate to choose either, depending on the kind of preparation he had received. The essential differences between the two lay in the fact that the Comprehensive Examination had no questions upon specifically designated readings in literature or upon English Grammar. A considerable majority of the Commission favored the Comprehensive Examination, but felt that they could not ignore conservative opinion. It was a period when English teachers were sharply divided in their preferences, and the report was obviously an attempt to satisfy everybody.

Under such conditions the Readers of the Comprehensive Examination took every precaution to avoid mistakes. In 1933 and 1934 the Chief Reader in English, Professor Jack R. Crawford, of Yale, held preliminary conferences with his table leaders, and the members of his Re-Read Committee spent much time determining standards and selecting sample answers. It was recognized that only by a consensus of judgments

could justice be done to candidates on a subjective examination. Probably never in the history of the Board
were papers scrutinized with more heed. There were
still "rugged individualists" among the Readers who
found it difficult to subordinate their own opinions to
the will of the group, but these Professor Crawford
managed to subdue. Even then, in spite of all that could
be done, some teachers read the results with a feeling
that justice had not been done to their pupils. Situations
of this sort paved the way for a modification of the
Board's examination philosophy.

The meetings of the English Readers had some
"comic relief" in the "boners" perpetrated by the ex-
aminees. Milton, in *Lycidas*, did not disdain "to inter-
pose a little ease"; and perhaps the Board's historian
will be forgiven if he lists at this point a few of the
more diverting specimens.

Macbeth is a typical husband, courageous and strong
when away from home.

He sees everything at once and writes them down in that
order.

Babbitt has a few of the old-fashioned graces, such as not
going to bed drunk every night.

The hound rushed over the moor, emitting whelps at
every leap.

Gabriel Oak, with all his horse sense, is really a stable
character.

He had reached the zenith of his apathy.

All the surrounding land was razed to the ground.

Let us call this boy Bill, for that was his name.

At birth he was a normal healthy child, who romped around with his little boy friends.

If he had not been so wavering, his own life, his mother's, and his lover's might have been avoided.

Soames was not too disappointed when he gave birth to a daughter, Fleur.

These are only a few of the hundreds of "boners" supplied by the Readers, and a volume of considerable size could be filled with similar contributions. In matters of this kind, every one has his own favorites, and some, I suspect, have been manufactured. The boy who replied to the question "Name two ancient sports" with the answer "Antony and Cleopatra" has been often quoted, but must be a fabulous character.

The story of what happened in the subject of History is still vivid in the memories of those who had a share in the discussion. In April, 1934, because of growing dissatisfaction with the existing tests, the Board again resorted to the appointment of a commission. The chairman was Professor Conyers Read, of the University of Pennsylvania, and among the members were several of the most distinguished scholars in that field: Professor James P. Baxter, III, then of Harvard and later President of Williams; Dr. Edmund E. Day, then of the Rockefeller Foundation, but afterwards President of Cornell; President Harold W. Dodds, of Princeton; Professor Carleton J. H. Hayes, of Columbia; Professor William L. Langer, of Harvard; Professor Wallace Notestein, of Yale; and several others. Probably the Board never assembled on any of its many commissions a group of educators of such high standing.

But when Professor Read presented the Commission report on October 27, 1936, violent disapprobation was at once indicated. The small tornado which followed its publication in the issue of *The Social Studies* for December, 1936, almost tore the Board apart. Professor Read and his associates had attempted to develop what they conceived to be a thoroughly "liberal" philosophy, emphasizing the weighing of evidence and not merely the repetition of factual material; but they quickly found that their ideas were far from widely popular. Even teachers who in their hearts approved of the theories advanced by the Commission recognized that their universal acceptance would be almost impossible.

Whether Professor Brigham, Professor Read, and the other leaders who were trying in all honesty to improve the Board examinations were right or wrong is not for this annalist to decide; but there can be little doubt that, in their enthusiasm, they neglected public sentiment and moved faster than some on the periphery of the Board were willing to go. Instructors who had taught History successfully for three or four decades and were justly proud of their reputations were suddenly asked to approve policies originating with a small group of research psychologists. They were suspicious, critical, and indignant. The marvel is that the reformers moved as far as they did.

What happened in the field of History was again in the nature of a compromise. At the spring meeting in 1938 the Board voted to offer in 1939 and thereafter two new examinations—a two-unit examination in English History and American History (History CD) and a two-unit examination in American History and Contemporary Civilization (History DE)—both to be alternative to the existing one-unit examinations. Unfortunately this interesting experiment proved to be a conspicuous failure. Teachers simply refused to prepare pupils for the two new tests. In 1939 only 26 candidates appeared for History CD and 31 for History DE. The figures in 1940 were no more encouraging, with 33 writing History CD and 31 History DE. When, in 1941, only 11 took History CD and 30 History DE, while 2,580 registered for the old one-unit examination in American History, it was apparent that the Old Order was still very healthy.

In 1940 still another commission, this time headed by President Baxter, made a careful survey of educational opinion and after much deliberation submitted revised requirements in the fields of Ancient, European, and English History, and a new requirement covering American History and Contemporary Civilization. In the January number of *Social Education* these suggestions were published, with requests for criticisms—and the criticisms rolled in. The eventual result was the withdrawal of these proposals, and things reverted to the *status quo*. Meanwhile war problems had claimed precedence in the Board's planning, and the introduction of a new type of achievement test in the Social Studies had altered the situation. Whether or not History teachers could have reached unanimity on aims and methods was never really demonstrated.

One has a feeling after pondering the reports of numerous Board Commissions at this period that teachers were groping earnestly for some magic formula which would guarantee accurate measurement of accomplishment. They had varying degrees of knowledge and wisdom, together with natural prejudices and whims, but they were zealous seekers after truth. That it evaded them will not astonish persons familiar with the complexity of the problem.

An illustration of what excitement may be aroused by a change apparently innocuous is the furore over "scaling." The Committee of Revision recommended in 1935 that the Committee on Examination Ratings consider the desirability of discontinuing the reporting of grades on the "percentage" scale from one to one hundred—which, to quote their words, "has given rise to the fictitious and fallacious 'passing mark' of 60 in the minds of teachers, parents, and pupils." Instead, they suggested, marks would be reported on the widely-accepted scale already familiar in the Scholastic Aptitude Test, which fixed the grade of the average college applicant at 500, distributed the scores so that they ranged from approximately 200 to 800, and yielded a continuous scale any point of which could be referred to the percentage of the random college admission population falling above and below it. Some resistance developed on the floor of the Board meeting, and final action was deferred until a poll could be taken. In reply to an explanatory memorandum 195 answers were favorable, 4 opposed, and 15 indifferent. After a careful analysis of the criticisms, the Board voted, on April 15, 1936, to put the new system into operation in 1937. Still the controversy was not over. When this action was reviewed by the Executive Committee in the following autumn, they warily decided to postpone the shift for

another year. This time, however, the full Board re
fused to delay any longer, and the new scale was employed in reporting all the examinations of June, 1937.

Much of the trouble in this case was due to misunderstanding and ignorance. In his report for 1937
Professor Mullins, speaking with the calm authority of
a mathematician, said very sensibly:

The way in which a grade is reported is not of great importance. The wide variety of grading systems now in use
is evidence that no one system has proved ideal. In general,
the trend is away from the percentage system. If a new
system is adopted, time at least is required before misin-
terpretations grow up about it. The system used by the
Board this year is one recommended by the technicians who
have studied the problem. It is the hope of the Board that
the difficulties of changing from an old and well established
system will not obscure the advantages of the new and less
familiar system.

The obstacles inherent in persuading Anglo-Saxons
to adopt the metric standard of measurement or to
modify the eccentricities of the Gregorian calendar are
well known. Even Theodore Roosevelt, with all his
prestige, could not force "simplified spelling" on the
American public. Logic has nothing to do with the
matter. To a considerable proportion of even intelligent people change is unwelcome. It is not astonishing,
then, that it took several years for teachers to become
accustomed to the new scale—or even to interpret it.

The ultimate success of many of the Board's new
policies should not lead anybody to minimize the
amount and fervor of the resistance to them. In 1936,
for example, the Country Day School Headmasters' As-

sociation took the lead in urging the Board to continue examinations for preliminary candidates and also to retain the "Old Plan restricted examinations." Sensitive, again, to educational opinion, the Board appointed a Special Committee, headed by Dr. Richard M. Gummere, of Harvard, to meet with representatives of this Association. These put up such a good case for themselves and their patrons that the Board at its next meeting passed a conciliatory resolution: "That the Board hereby reaffirms its confidence in the soundness of the procedures underlying the Mathematics Attainment Test and strongly recommends its use, but that, as a special service to a group of secondary schools, the restricted examination in Mathematics . . . be continued for a period of two years after 1938."

On the other hand, great credit must be assigned to Professor Brigham and his colleagues for their skill in disarming opposition. No matter how much he may have fumed inside, he was never dogmatic or supercilious. Sometimes he moved too rapidly. Occasionally, like some other research men, he allowed his dreams to sway his judgment. But few liberal reformers have seen their hopes more fully realized in a short space of time.

The financial status of an educational board is neither irrelevant nor unimportant. The College Entrance Examination Board had a responsibility to the member institutions by which it was created. If its deficit was too large, the management was liable to attack. Fortunately, in spite of a declining number of patrons, the Board had weathered the financial storms of the 1930's without even nearing the shoals of insolvency. In 1928, while the Great Boom was still under way, the excess of receipts over disbursements was $21,173.99, and in 1929 it was $14,332.54. By this date the annual budget had grown to more than $250,000, and the Board was in the category of Big Business. Even in 1930, a sad year for industry, the profit on operations—if it may be called that—amounted to $15,203.45, and the Custodians' Account was still mounting. In 1931, it is true, the Board had a slight operating deficit of $216.96, but rigid economies were promptly started, and in 1933 it was again "in the black" for $6,784.49. In 1935 the Board's profit was $1,329.59, but it must be noted that the budget in that year had been reduced to $175,000. By that time the approximate value of the securities held by the Custodians had risen to almost $200,000.

These statistics, bare in themselves, prove that the Board executives had managed well, arranging to reduce expenses as the revenue from fees declined. Moreover, they had put aside from year to year a modest reserve for contingencies. On this point the Secretary wrote in 1938:

The financial condition of the Board is satisfactory. Although the Board has no endowment, the invested fund held by the Custodians serves as a protection against any minor emergency. While the Custodians' Fund should be increased from time to time, it seems wiser at this juncture to use additional yearly income over and above the current expenses to expand the Board's services or to adjust and reduce fees whenever possible. First consideration is being given to the question as to whether or not the finances of the Board will permit some reduction in fees.

There was some reason for the Secretary to be troubled over the matter of the fee, for the cost per candidate had risen from $7.98 in 1922 to $9.97 in 1926 and $11.09 in 1929. Through the early 1930's this item remained fairly stable, being $10.74 in 1928 and $10.87 in 1932. The cost of the first Scholastic Aptitude Test, in 1926, was $2.48 for each registrant.

From the crisis of 1929 and the ensuing depression, then, the Board emerged with nothing more serious than a falling-off in the market value of its invested funds. Its management was sound and economical. It was under no necessity of raising its fees for candidates or reducing its *honoraria* to its Examiners and Readers. Its expenditures for research mounted, of course, with the development of the Scholastic Aptitude Test and the opening of the laboratories at Princeton, but these were taken care of through the normal sources of revenue.

Until the First World War the Board continued to occupy rent-free quarters provided by Columbia University—first in the University Library and later in University Hall and Hamilton Hall. In 1916, however, it rented a house at 431 West 117th Street, only a few doors from its present headquarters and convenient to the Columbia campus. The Readers worked in rooms in both Columbia and Barnard—wherever space could be found—and ate their meals first in "Mrs. Prince's Dining Room" and afterwards in the Columbia Commons. During the busy season, from June to August, it was necessary to find accommodations for the Board's special staff of clerical assistants; and year after year Columbia, Barnard, or Union Theological Seminary came to the rescue. It was all very hectic, and each spring the problem of seeking rooms had to be confronted anew.

The Secretary pointed out in 1927 that the Board, in order to have adequate facilities, was then renting three buildings in New York and one in Princeton. The heady wine of Coolidge prosperity led the Board to appoint a committee, headed by Miss Woolley, to solicit funds for the erection of a six-story structure on a site approximately sixty by a hundred feet in a very desirable location. By this date the Board had a permanent staff of sixteen under one roof, and employed also 85 Examiners, 699 Readers, 804 Supervisors and Proctors, and 107 temporary clerks and assistants. So far as can be ascertained, the committee never made a report, and the advent of 1929, with its attendant financial panic, effectually blocked any plans for a building solely devoted to College Entrance Examination Board purposes. The right moment never came.

Professor Mullins made his first report as Secretary in September, 1937. With much satisfaction he announced that during the year the Board's Scholastic Aptitude Test and Mathematics Attainment Test had been placed at the disposal of the Committee of Graduate Deans of Harvard, Yale, Princeton, and Columbia for use in their Graduate Record Examination taken by advanced students. The Board's Research and Statistical Laboratory in Princeton had assisted the Secondary Education Board in preparing and scoring what was called the Junior Scholastic Aptitude Test. In co-operation with the New Jersey Commission for the Blind, the Research Secretary had prepared a special Braille edition of the Scholastic Aptitude Test. He had also completed for the Department of State a study of the scores of all candidates taking the examinations for the consular service in 1937.

Of more significance than any of these steps was the initiation, at the request of Harvard, Yale, and Princeton, of a series of examinations to be held early in the spring for the testing of competitors for scholarships. On April 24, 1937, at 118 centers located throughout the United States, 2,005 competitors were examined. In the morning they took a form of the Scholastic Aptitude Test consisting of two parts, one testing verbal aptitude and one testing mathematical aptitude. In the afternoon they took an achievement test prepared by the Cooperative Test Service of the American Council on Education. Furthermore, the Board authorized, at its meeting on April 14, 1937, certain early examinations for admission, to be established at the request and for the benefit of a number of colleges which had hitherto made little use of the June series. These were to be held on the same date and at the same centers as the scholarship examinations and included a foreign language test and a form of the Scholastic Aptitude Test with both a verbal and a mathematical section. It was pointed out by Professor Mullins that the series was organized "primarily for institutions that wish to complete the selection of their freshman classes earlier in the year than is possible if they depend upon the results of the examinations taken at the regular June session." Here was framed the pattern which, as we shall see, was to become during wartime the permanent policy of the Board. In undertaking this interesting experiment, both Professor Brigham and Professor Mullins had undoubtedly an eye on the future.

The new Secretary presented his own conception of the functions and ideals of the Board, as follows:

During the last quarter of a century there has been a growing interest in examination and testing procedures. Many individuals, educational institutions, and business agencies have contributed to the development of a wide variety of tests in an effort to discover measuring devices of greater meaning and dependability. In such a flux of ideas pertaining to examinations the Board has a multiple task to perform. In the first place, it has to carry forward its services of developing examinations, administering them at its supervised centers, and grading the papers. It must utilize what it feels to be the best procedures at the moment. In the second place, it must follow with a reasoned criticalness the important new developments in examining techniques, and be alert in adapting established improvements to its own ends. Finally the Board must make its own contribution to the field of examinations. To strengthen examinations and tests which are of promising value and to give a valid interpretation to them is no easy task. The examinations of to-day are not like those of twenty-five years ago, and there is no good reason to believe that the examinations of the future will be exactly like those of the present.

The prestige of any representative organization like the College Entrance Examination Board depends, of course, on its leaders. It has long been composed of forceful personalities, each one accustomed to dominate in his or her own bailiwick, and each with a peculiar institutional consciousness and devotion. Some are ready and fluent in argument; others are more taciturn, but in the long run no less influential. Some, because of their stability and trustworthiness, are particularly relied upon when crises arise or sane decisions are required. The meetings of committees and commissions have brought about the mingling of minds, accompanied by clashes of opinion mixed with good-natured raillery. Persons afflicted with provincial dogmatism have emerged from these contacts chastened in spirit and a trifle dubious about their own infallibility.

Professor Fiske was accustomed to boast that the ablest members of the teaching profession had been drafted for service as Examiners and Readers. Among those cited in his final report were President Bowman, of Johns Hopkins, President Comfort, of Haverford, President Compton, of the Massachusetts Institute of Technology, President Conant, of Harvard (who was an Examiner in Chemistry in 1925), President Davis, of Stevens Institute, and President Neilson, of Smith. He mentioned also Professor Wilbur L. Cross, of Yale (later Governor of Connecticut), some twenty members of the National Academy of Science, and many others recognized as authorities in the respective fields. Professor Mullins, writing in 1938, also paid his tribute to the group when he said: "A review of the records for the last thirty-eight years reveals the extent to which eminent teachers and scholars have given their time to the work of the various commissions that have brought about needed changes in the examination program."

It is not an exaggeration to say that no educational enterprise, over a long period of years, has brought together a more impressive body of teachers and administrators.

In the affairs of the Board a few of the members of long standing continued to be active through the 1930's. President Butler, although his interest had not waned, was serving a wider public; but Dr. Farrand stood out in the meetings like Nestor, and President Ferry and Professor Corwin were Elder Statesmen, keeping the past alive for the benefit of the present and the future. New voices, also, were being raised and heard. Several heads of women's colleges were very active in the councils of the Board: Dean Virginia C. Gildersleeve, of Barnard, with her incisive mind and forceful manner; President Marion E. Park, of Bryn Mawr, brisk, business-like, and witty; President Ada Lee Comstock (now Mrs. Wallace Notestein), of Radcliffe, a thoughtful and friendly Olympian; Dean C. Mildred Thompson, of Vassar, with her gift for effective summarization; and after 1936 Miss Mildred McAfee (now Mrs. Douglas Horton), of Wellesley, blending practicality with graciousness and charm. Harvard, Yale, and Princeton were inclined to leave their Board affairs in charge of their directors of admission; accordingly, Dr. Gummere, Mr. Noyes, and Dean Heermance spoke with the sanction of their powerful institutions behind them. Among others who did much more than their share were Miss Margaret T. Corwin, Dean of the New Jersey College for Women and the brilliant daughter of Professor Corwin; Miss Margaret S. Morriss, Dean of Pembroke College; Dr. J. Edgar Park, of Wheaton College, whose whimsical Irish humor was always welcome in debate; Dean E. Gordon Bill, of Dartmouth, blunt, courageous, and uncompromising; President Bancroft Beatley, of Simmons, who in any discussion was a steadying influence; and always in the background President Neilson, inscrutable, watchful, with a devastating facility in argument and rebuttal. These are only a few of the many who, in the retrospect, seem to have controlled the destinies of the Board.

The secondary school representatives, excepting Dr. Farrand, were likely to be a little diffident in full Board meetings, but their advice was indispensable on committees. Among those who made the greatest contribution were W. L. W. Field, of Milton Academy; Paul E. Elicker, of Newton High School; Ralph E. Files, of East Orange; Miss Mira B. Wilson, of Northfield Seminary; and William C. Hill, of the Classical High School, Springfield, Massachusetts.

The Executive Committee and the other controlling committees—the Committee of Review, the Committee on Examination Ratings, the Committee on Examination Schedules, and the Committee of Revision— took their duties very seriously. Gradually the practice had grown up of holding meetings of standing committees on Tuesdays, in the fall and spring, followed by an assembly of the full Board on Wednesday morning. After this would come a luncheon, with a speaker or two on some current educational topic.

Although participation was in theory open to everybody, it was not often that questions of importance were threshed out on the floor of the Board meetings. Usually the investigation had been accomplished by smaller groups, whose recommendations had then been passed upon by the well-informed Executive Committee. The Chairman and the Executive Secretary certainly welcomed an interchange of opinions, but the preliminary work had usually been so thorough that not much could be added. Once in a while, however, Dean Bill or President Beatley would ask pertinent questions, or President Neilson, an undaunted supporter of the essay type of question in subjects such as English or History, would rise to cross-examine the young psychologists who were attacking it; and then the sparks would fly. The number of mere "yes-men" and "echo-women" on the Board has always been small.

The philosophy and practice of the Board had been altered in the 1930's with so much tact and skill that few outsiders, and even some of the members, did not fully realize what had taken place. One by one old procedures were quietly dropped and new ones took their place. The Board of 1938 was something very different from that of thirty years before. When the Second World War created unexpected needs for testing millions of young men, the Board—thanks to its recent modernization—was ready, without any wasteful delay, to meet the emergency.

CHAPTER VII

AND THEN
CAME
THE WAR

IN THE RETROSPECT the Board meetings during the years just before the Second World War seem lively and thrilling. Imaginative minds had taken hold of its operations. At committee luncheons the research workers from the Princeton laboratories were using technical terms which mystified the laymen. Nobody was afraid of new ideas, and a tonic pioneer spirit pervaded the discussions. The three specialists who led the advance were, of course, Professor Brigham (Research Secretary), Mr. Stalnaker (Consultant Examiner), and Professor Mullins (Executive Secretary). The Chairman from 1936 to 1939, following Dean Heermance, was Dr. Richard M. Gummere, of Harvard. A graduate of Haverford College in 1902, he took his doctorate at Harvard in 1907, became a teacher of Latin at Haverford, and was Headmaster of the William Penn Charter School in Philadelphia from 1918 to 1935, when he accepted the directorship of admissions at Harvard. Even as headmaster he had been actively a worker on Board committees, and it is not remarkable that he was chosen Chairman after having been a college representative for only one year. A classical scholar of distinction and broad culture, Dr. Gummere preserves a happy balance between conservatism and exploration, and his humanistic love of traditions has never inhibited his genuine liberalism. With his background and training he was just the person to supplement the thinking of three expert scientists such as Professors Brigham, Stalnaker, and Mullins.

Marion E. Park, who in 1939 succeeded Dr. Gummere as Chairman, also came from a family of educators and was steeped in the Greek and Roman classics. She had been made President of Bryn Mawr in 1922, after administrative experience at Simmons and Radcliffe, and knew thoroughly the peculiar problems of the women's colleges. Direct, very articulate and keen-witted, she kept her poise even in the midst of responsibilities brought about by the coming of war to the United States.

Who were the other leaders of the Board during that prewar period? Dr. Farrand, still provocative, ubiquitous, and helpful, was chairman of the Committee on Examination Ratings, and also Chief Custodian; President J. Edgar Park, of Wheaton, was chairman of the Committee on Examination Schedules; and the chairman of the very important Committee of Revision was Dean Frances L. Knapp, of Wellesley, an indefatigable worker and a wise counsellor. On the Executive Committee were familiar figures, notable for their reliability: President Ferry and Professor Corwin, Dean Heermance, President Neilson, and Dean C. Mildred Thompson, along with Dr. Joseph Dana Allen, of Polytechnic Preparatory Country Day School, in Brooklyn, and Paul E. Elicker, of Newton, Massachusetts. To any newcomer in the group, the presence of these distinguished personalities, so different in their viewpoints but so constructive and forward-looking, was very stimulating. They were united in their insistence that the Board should not just "play safe," but should move out boldly to meet the needs of a younger generation.

The Scholastic Aptitude Test, with all its implications, had already fixed the pattern for the Board's modern program, and around it was focused most of the comment, favorable and unfavorable, on its decisions. For more than a decade since 1926, when the Test was first offered, the number of candidates who submitted themselves to it, either by itself or in combination with other examinations, had remained fairly steady. In 1937 they numbered 9,272, of whom 2,633 took the Scholastic Aptitude Test only. Needless to say, it was being watched from year to year, sometimes approvingly, sometimes critically. The colleges were being more and more impressed by its practical value. In 1939, for example, it was used as a validating examination for applicants for West Point, and admissions officers in institutions which had not hitherto cared much for the Board were beginning to speak of it with respect. Clearly it was proving to be a popular feature of the Board's laboratory products. There was even danger that the general public might spoil everything by regarding it as a magical means of measurement.

As the Scholastic Aptitude Test gained in favor, there was also a growing feeling that examinations for admission might well be pushed back to an earlier date, perhaps even as far as April. Many colleges had long been

desirous of notifying their applicants before late July—
the earliest practicable time under the existing schedule.
The June examinations, occupying a full week after
most schools had closed, had assumed too much importance in the lives of boys and girls. The April series of
tests, introduced mainly as an experiment in 1937 for
the benefit of scholarship competitors and covering only
one day, had been highly satisfactory for that specific
purpose and had even been used by several colleges as
validating material for candidates for admission. Thus,
without any pressure from the Board, the June registration slowly commenced to shrink and the April registration to increase. In 1939, perceiving the trend and
eager to please its customers, the Board removed all
restrictions limiting the Scholastic Achievement Tests
to the use of competitors for scholarships, and they were
then available for admission purposes as well.

The total registration in 1940 was the largest since
1930 in the history of the Board—which, incidentally,
was also serving a larger number of colleges than in any
previous year. The most significant phenomenon, however, was the rise in the April registration in four years
from 2,005 to 10,318. In commenting on this gratifying
expansion, Professor Mullins wrote: "The increased
use of the Board's tests and examinations is partly due to
the flexibility of the examining program. The schools
and colleges have a choice between the April and June
series, or a combination of both."

The truth is that admissions officers, always on the
lookout for improved measuring devices, were losing
their former skepticism about the prognostic value of
the Scholastic Aptitude Test and the April Achieve-

ment Tests. Briefly, the Scholastic Aptitude Test at this date consisted of two sections, one on verbal aptitude and one on mathematical aptitude. The Achievement Test program included separate tests of one hour each in Social Studies; in reading knowledge of French, German, Latin, and Spanish; in science knowledge of Biology, Chemistry, and Physics; and in Spatial Relations. A candidate was allowed to take one, two, or at a maximum three of the Achievement Tests, his choice of subjects depending on the advice of the college to which he was seeking admission. All the tests were scored mechanically and expeditiously by clerks.

As the use of the tests spread, the experts were observing attentively the merits and demerits of the system which they had created. Limited to a single day, or at most a day and a half, the April tests were necessarily brief and largely objective. They did interrupt somewhat the routine of the school year, and this annoyed teachers who liked order and continuity. Many teachers could not understand how tests taken before all the material of a "course" had been covered, could be of any substantial value. These objections had to be answered, and are still being answered in some quarters even to-day. On the other hand, there did seem to be an unusually high correlation between their results and the grades which the candidates later secured at college. If the colleges could get the information which they required in a shorter time, more accurately, and at less expense, were not these advantages worth considering? Mr. Stalnaker, commenting in 1941 on the April tests, expressed his personal view, but was careful, as always, not to claim too much.

The purpose of the April series of tests, stated in its briefest form, is to provide information which the users of the series will find a valuable supplement to the other data they have about the candidates applying for scholarships or for admission. The ratings on the tests should help a college in determining which students will probably be successful in that college, and which are most likely to be the distinguished students to whom scholarships should be given. The test results should also prove of use in placement and guidance work after the candidate has been admitted to the institution.

That the tests are reasonably successful in these regards is suggested by their increasing use. Every step in the development, the administration, and the scoring of the tests, and in the reporting of the results, is taken with the end in view of increasing their value to the colleges. But the exact degree of the success of the tests is not easily determined. Each institution quite rightly makes its own use of the tests, and their value may very well vary from institution to institution. It is to be hoped that the colleges will study the effectiveness of the tests for their own purposes, for through such study ways may be found to make the tests still more helpful predictive instruments. The program is a flexible one, and may be altered to meet the requirements of the users.

This statement, so restrained, so candid, and so entirely devoid of extravagant claims, is indicative of the scrupulous integrity with which the Board's research staff surveyed their work.

In 1940, when the crisis in European affairs seemed likely to embroil the United States, the Board offered to the Federal Government such of its services as might assist the country's defense; and the Secretary of War appointed Professor Brigham as an expert consultant to advise the War Department in matters pertaining to the classification of commissioned and enlisted personnel. After its regrettable unpreparedness in the First World War, the War Department did not propose to be caught unawares, without plans for classification down on paper, available for any contingency.

At the opening of the year 1941, however, everything was serene in the Board's offices and laboratories. The officers of the Board, enjoying a lull after turmoil, were in a mood to pause for contemplation. The previous autumn meeting had been uneventful, and no major changes in policy were in the offing. Then came that Sunday afternoon in December when the news of Pearl Harbor blared out over the radio, to the surprise even of the President of the United States and to the consternation of millions of Americans. When our Declaration of War followed, the officials of the Board promptly determined, like most of our citizens, to turn ploughshares into swords and to make its machinery as effective in war as it had been in peace. Within their special province there was much which they could do to help. In his report for 1942, Professor Mullins wrote:

No narrow view should be taken at the present time of the Board's work and function; useful and practical considerations should be the determining factor in shaping its policies. Broad plans for greater cooperation in the future between school and college need not be discarded, but these should be put in the background. Every effort must now be centered on the present with help for the war effort as the paramount concern.

This voiced the mood of the Board during the war years—a period during which, as President Dixon Ryan

Fox once said, the word "usual" disappeared from the American vocabulary. Before many months had passed, the Research and Statistical Laboratories at Princeton were engaged in at least five different new projects for the government and for related scientific groups.

Even before the outbreak of the war with Japan and Germany, some of the largest users of the June examinations had been seriously considering their abandonment and the employment in their stead of the shorter and earlier April tests. On Sunday, December 7, Dean Heermance had invited to Princeton Dr. Gummere and Mr. Noyes for an informal conference of what their friends called The Three Musketeers, together with Dr. Mullins, who gracefully played the part of D'Artagnan. As they chatted before the wood fire in Heermance's study before luncheon, he announced that Princeton might shortly turn to the April tests as better suited to her admission pattern. Gummere and Noyes were in sympathy with the idea, but were not quite sure that the hour had arrived for what might be regarded as a radical departure from tradition. The conversation was lively, and the men indulged in their customary casual "digs" at one another and their respective institutions. Nobody had any premonition of what was imminent.

As the quartette sat smoking after luncheon, Heermance was called to the telephone, and his guests could not help hearing him cry excitedly and repeatedly, "Well, I'll be be damned!" He returned with the news of Pearl Harbor; and the four agreed then and there that an entire change in the Board's program could not be avoided. Early Monday morning the Princeton administrative group met with President Harold W.

Dodds; and while that discussion was in progress, Gummere and Noyes telephoned their colleges, so that they were in a strategic position to make plans for the immediate present and to outline a course of action for the future. Later the three men, with Mullins's co-operation, prepared and shortly released to the newspapers an announcement to be published on Thursday, December 18. The first two paragraphs, under the heading "Harvard, Princeton, and Yale Announce War-Time Changes in Curriculum and Plans of Admission," read as follows:

The three universities will move together to a war-time footing. Provision will be made for year-round instruction, so as to accelerate training of those students who may be called to service. In all three universities, studies will continue throughout the summer. Further announcements of details will be made separately by the three universities.

In order to make possible early selection of the next entering class, so that Freshmen who wish to participate in the accelerated curriculum may be ready to start work in late June or early July, Harvard, Princeton, and Yale announce, for the duration of the emergency, a plan by which applicants may be notified of admission early in May. As before, chief weight will be laid on the applicants' records in secondary school. As validating tests, the three universities will use, for most applicants, the April series provided by the College Entrance Examination Board. These tests consist of the Scholastic Aptitude Test on the morning of Saturday, April 11, and a series of achievement tests in languages, sciences, and social sciences, on that afternoon. Choice among these latter tests will depend upon the student's preparatory courses in his final school year and his plans for college.

As soon as this situation was clarified, Professor Mullins called Miss Park, the Chairman of the Board, who promptly declared that Bryn Mawr and possibly some of the other colleges for women might like to join the movement. One or two of the presidents of the women's colleges were not at first in sympathy with the idea, feeling that they were being stampeded into radicalism. Within a short period, however, the seven largest of them reached a common agreement. It was thus possible for the Executive Secretary to estimate that of the approximately 10,000 boys and girls who had planned to write the June essay examinations in 1942, at least 6,500 would now be transferred to the April tests. Even of the remaining 3,500, there was doubt as to how many would appear for the June series. What happened was no startling surprise to those who had been watching educational trends. But Dean Heermance writes: "It is my personal opinion that it would have been a long hard fight to have gained a complete support for our present objectives had they not been introduced as a war-time measure."

Professor Stalnaker, as Consultant Examiner, immediately prepared a memorandum stating that in his judgment it would be unwise at that late date to attempt to make any alterations in the announced program for April, 1942. All that would be necessary would be the printing of a larger number of papers. To this the Executive Committee quickly gave their approval; and then, on December 22, they took the further sensational step of voting to substitute for the series of examinations already announced for June, 1942, a series similar to that arranged for April, with the addition of Part I of the Mathematics Attainment Test. A special edition of the *New Bulletin* was hurried out to the more than five thousand schools and colleges making use of the Board's services, and every detail was carried through as originally planned.

The flexibility of the Board and its capacity for emergency adjustment were demonstrated by the speed and audacity with which it took action. It is true that it had been gradually, though often unconsciously, heading in that direction for several years and that Professors Mullins and Brigham had said privately to one another, "Eventually—why not now?" But any suggestion that the June examination week be abandoned would normally have been resented in conservative quarters. It was undoubtedly preferable to have circumstances force it on school and college communities than to have it come through a close vote after acrimonious discussion. The war merely expedited what was already inevitable. The matter of timing was settled by Japan and Germany.

All the publicity had insisted that this sensational action had been precipitated by the national crisis, and schoolmasters were soon asking, "Will the regular June series of examinations be restored when the war is over?" Professor Stalnaker, in his memorandum, said quietly, "There is an appreciable probability that the present type of June program will never regain sufficient numbers to permit its continuation." The inner circle of the Board had really little doubt. Indeed, the Executive Secretary, in his report for 1942, remarked: "The passing of the June essay-type examination after continuous use for forty-one years marks the end of an era so far as the history of the Board is concerned." The number taking the April tests in 1942 was 16,626 as compared with 10,799 the year before. Of these, 5,326 registered for the Scholastic Aptitude Test only, and 11,300 for the complete series.

Nevertheless, the "scrapping" of the June essay examinations was regretted in many quarters. English instructors especially were fearful that the discontinuation of the three-hour comprehensive examination in their subject would react unfavorably on the teaching of literature in schools. In rebuttal, Professor Stalnaker, now Associate Secretary, wrote in 1943, with a dogmatism unusual for him:

The type of test so highly valued by teachers of English, which requires the candidate to write a theme or essay, is not a worth-while testing device. Whether or not the writing of essays as a means of teaching writing deserves the place it has in the secondary school curriculum may be equally questioned. Eventually, it is hoped, sufficient evidence may be accumulated to outlaw forever the "write-a-theme-on" . . . type of examination.

Against this doctrine, so positively stated, the protests were vehement, particularly from scholars such as President Neilson and others, who were not easily silenced. In 1942 a number of institutions which thought highly of the essay-type examinations requested the Board to consider the possibility of continuing them, if not for college admission, at least as terminal examinations for secondary schools. Although the cost of such a program seemed prohibitive, the Board did, as an experimental concession, authorize the use in June, 1942, of the question papers in English and in American History already prepared by the Examiners. Each school agreed to be responsible for administering the examinations and reading the papers. It is significant that more than two hundred schools from all parts of the country subscribed to the plan and that the approximate number of question papers distributed was 10,000 for the English and 6,500 for the American History. Not even the *obiter dicta* of professional researchers could suppress the widespread conviction that the writing of an essay offered valuable evidence as to a pupil's ability to use and understand his own language.

The defenders of this belief virtually forced the Board to add in 1943 a one-hour test in English Composition to the group of achievement tests; and at the urgent request of a group of engineering schools, a four-year comprehensive test in Mathematics was permitted as a substitute for the Gamma section of the Mathematics Attainment Test. These two examinations were, in 1943, the only ones requiring professional Readers. In April, 1943, forty Readers were employed for the English Composition Test and three Readers for the Comprehensive Mathematics Test. All the others were scored by automata. It was in striking contrast with the old days when an army of Readers invaded Morningside Heights each June, looking forward with anticipation to a reunion with old friends.

Whatever advantages the mechanical system possessed—and they were many—there was an irreparable loss in the removal of the "Reader link" between the teachers in schools and those in colleges. It has more than once been pointed out that the "reading period" in June had offered for years an opportunity for the exchange of ideas among teachers in the same field, and had carried them out of their local ruts into the broad thoroughfare of educational thinking. They did work hard in a hot city, but they went back refreshed and much better informed as to trends. The position of Reader had come to be regarded as a privilege and an honor; and those who had held it could hardly be enthusiastic about any impersonal system of measuring the results of months of classroom teaching.

As a by-no-means-adequate substitute, the Board started in 1941 a series of informal conferences at which groups of school and college representatives could meet with Board officials and listen to explanations of what was occurring. For example, on March 4, 1941, representatives of schools which sent 100 or more candidates to the 1940 examinations met in New York City to discuss various phases of the Board's policies. This was particularly valuable because it brought into direct contact with the Board school men and women not ordinarily associated with its committees and commissions. As an experiment in human relations, it was most successful. Later gatherings of a similar type served as a means of healthful and legitimate indoctrination.

At a moment when aptitude and achievement tests were assuming so much importance, it was natural that college faculties should be inquiring into their validity. The experts themselves, in their laboratories at Princeton, were put on their mettle and were anxious to anticipate possible criticism. In 1944 Professor Stalnaker, having declared that such activity was gratifying and should be encouraged, went on to express the hope that investigators would be willing to recognize "the complexities of an exact study of selection and placement and the many important factors involved which do not readily lend themselves to analysis." He continued: "Low correlations between test scores and course grades do not necessarily indicate that a change in the tests is desirable. Several other factors must also be considered."

Experienced admissions officers, of course, already knew this, and the best of them formed their judgments not only from the College Entrance Examination Board results but also from the candidate's school record and from the Headmaster's confidential report. On the basis of this information a good admissions officer had learned to prepare a prognosis chart, which was often astonishingly accurate, taking into consideration character, motivation, personal habits, heredity, environment, and other items which the Board, even with the best of intentions, has never been able to measure. Professor Stalnaker was emphasizing a truism when he wrote: "Test scores can be completely understood only if the background and the future plans of the candidates are considered in addition to the nature of the test. A mere multiplicity of test scores solves few problems."

One step of considerable significance was taken in 1942, when the Board for the first time sent to the schools for their confidential use the approximate scores on the achievement tests of their students who were final candidates for college. This procedure, involving only some extra bookkeeping, was much appreciated, for it permitted helpful comparisons between schools, between departments in the same school, and between teachers in the same department. Thus, an instructor was able in some degree to check his own work as well as that of his pupils.

In the autumn of 1942 Dr. Karl G. Miller, Dean of the College of Liberal Arts for Women at the University of Pennsylvania, succeeded Miss Park as Chairman and presided over the Board's activities for the remainder of the war period. A graduate of the University of Pennsylvania in the Class of 1915, he served in the First World War and then took his doctorate in Psychology. In 1926 he became Director of Admissions at Pennsylvania, and a year later he was promoted to a full professorship. His experience as soldier, scholar, and administrator equipped him perfectly to make the almost daily decisions demanded by the emergency.

What these decisions were is vivid in the memories of many living members of the Board. Because of the war needs, the Research Laboratory was subjected to an almost incredible expansion. Professor Stalnaker was at once loaned to the government and became the instigator and center of countless activities connected with the selection and assignment of personnel. His titles were numerous and impressive. He was first appointed Chairman of the Committee on Service Personnel—Selection and Training, under the National Research Council, Division of Anthropology and Psychology. Shortly afterwards he was named by the Secretary of the Navy to serve on a Committee of Three to survey certain aspects of the naval training program. Here was a chance for the educational psychologists to try out on an unprecedented scale their modern testing material.

Professor Mullins recognized this when he wrote in 1942: "In the selection process now in use for the armed forces and for the war industries, thousands of men and women will be taking tests, the results of which will be used to determine the fitness of the person and the most suitable place for him in service or industry."

It seemed almost as if the College Entrance Examination Board had been getting ready during the previous five or six years for precisely this contingency, and it had reason to be proud of the efficiency and speed with which its research staff met successive government requirements. Early in 1943 the regular sources of junior-officer material for a rapidly expanding navy seemed to be approaching exhaustion, and it was obvious that some fair and democratic process must be devised for screening candidates from the army of high-school seniors shortly to be graduated. Commander Alvin C. Eurich, then Officer-in-Charge of the Standards and Curriculum Section of the Navy Training Division, was assigned the problem of working out the detailed procedures for the preliminary selection of the men to be considered. He and his associates quickly decided that this could not be done through ordinary government channels and accordingly turned to Professor Stalnaker, who was named General Director of the proposed Testing Program. Here was the inception of the famous V-12 tests, destined to become so familiar—and so awesome—to eighteen-year-old American youth. The object was to select from a large body of boys with high-school training those best qualified to meet responsibility and be commissioned as officers; it was felt that many of the same attributes which would entitle men to admission to college would make them good leaders in war.

On February 27, 1943, the Board's Executive Committee adopted a budget sufficient to meet the cost of the proposed Navy testing, and when the Army joined the project, in March, the original budget had to be considerably enlarged. Shortly Henry Chauncey, then Assistant to the Dean of the Faculty of Arts and Sciences at Harvard, was appointed Assistant Director, under Professor Stalnaker. On April 2, 1943, came the much-advertised Great Day, when at more than 13,000 centers in high schools and colleges the V-12 and A-12 tests were administered to approximately 316,000 young men. Ten national regions had been set up under ten Regional Directors, with thousands of school and college teachers acting as supervisors. The College Entrance Examination Board had agreed to act as the coordinating and planning agency. It prepared the test and printed and distributed to all schools the information about the program and the order forms required. The nature of the content and the general form of the test had been dictated by the navy after consultation with technicians of the Board. It was the Board which furnished the machinery and the facilities for carrying the plan to completion. The Executive Secretary was justified in saying, "Never before in the history of testing has so large and able a group of experts been assembled to concentrate their skill and talents on so important and vast a problem relating to a homogeneous and uniform group."

This first Army-Navy Qualifying Test was regarded

by the armed forces as highly successful. It was followed by a similar program, on November 9, 1943, at which 78,000 were registered, and by still another, on March 14, 1944, with 170,000 candidates. In all three the accumulated experience of the Board in supervised testing served as a guide and provided the working pattern. Indeed, when it was all over Professor Stalnaker said: "The services which were supplied to the Army and Navy in war are essentially the same services provided for the schools and colleges in peace, and for this reason the Board faces no reconversion problems." It is important to keep in mind that the war work of the Board was, on a larger scale, only a continuation and expansion of what it had been accomplishing in the late 1930's.

In the year 1943–44, with war personnel demands at their height, the Board reached an "all-time high" in its expansion. For strictly college applicants it offered its usual four series of tests to a total of 26,166 candidates, the largest number in its forty-four years. It also, as we have seen, directed the general operation of the second and third Army-Navy College Qualifying Tests for high school seniors and graduates. Moreover, it supplied, under the direction of the Bureau of Navy Personnel, tests for 65,000 men in the second year of the Navy V-12 program. The Board actually handled all the routine work connected with these testing programs, from the development of the questions through pretesting, preparation of instructions for administration, preparation of final copy, printing, packaging, and shipping the tests, preparation of instructions for administration, receiving the material back from colleges, scoring, reporting, and studying the results. Under one single contract the Board handled for the Bureau of Naval Personnel approximately one hundred service jobs, including the printing or reprinting of 133 tests, answer sheets, and bulletins—a total of 36,000,000 pages of material.

These stupendous feats could not have been accomplished without considerably increasing the expert personnel. In addition to Mr. Chauncey, who spent seventeen months with the Board while on leave from Harvard, Dr. Harold O. Gulliksen was brought from the University of Illinois to carry on and supervise numerous scholarly research studies. The Board also employed several psychologists and test technicians to whom special duties were assigned. At the close of 1944 the professional staff included eighteen, of whom twelve had a doctor's degree; and according to Professor Stalnaker their influence revitalized the research office. After praising their achievements, he drew attention to the necessity of an able, well-trained, and aggressive staff if an effective examining program were to be maintained in the future. Productive research and experimental ventures were, he asserted, essential if the Board was to uphold its position of leadership and justify the interest, attention, and support of the colleges which had joined together to create it. This was only one of the many lessons learned during the war.

In addition to these major projects, the Board undertook some fascinating minor ones lying "on the fringe of the central purpose for which it was founded." In October, 1944, it authorized the preparation of an Aptitude Test for returning veterans seeking admission to college. It furnished the tests qualifying candidates for scholarships awarded by the Westinghouse Electric and Manufacturing Company. It prepared and administered for the first time in 1945 a special aptitude test for the nation-wide scholarship program established by the Pepsi-Cola Company—a program under which, on April 16, 1945, a total of 14,584 students were tested in 3,729 schools. It continued to assist the Department of State in preparing and scoring examinations used in the selection of personnel for the Foreign Service. After having administered a battery of tests to each incoming class at the United States Naval Academy, at Annapolis, it was finally, in 1946, asked to prepare and score all the entrance examinations to that institution; and it was requested at about the same time, although quite independently, to assist in preparing the entrance examinations for the Coast Guard Academy. The Board seemed to be getting not only bigger and bigger, but also better and better.

The financial condition of the Board over this war period remained eminently satisfactory. The elimination of the June essay examinations, which had been very expensive to read, reduced the running expenses from $40,744.96, in 1941, to $7,659.86, in 1942. In the fiscal year 1941–42, when the excess of operating income over expenditures was $44,885.83, the fee for the Scholastic Aptitude Test was reduced from five dollars to four and that for any other single test or combination of tests from ten dollars to eight. About this time the work for the Government began, and it was carried out on a "true cost" basis, with its activities assuming their proportion of fixed overhead charges as well as sharing in the use of the Board's equipment, quarters, and office personnel. Naturally, receipts and expenditures were both on a large scale. The Report for the fiscal year ending September 30, 1944, for example, showed a total operating income of $529,038.40 against costs of $491,456.55—figures which startled the Executive Committee. Without any expectation of profiting by its war enterprises, the Board saw its resources rapidly mounting, and the Custodians' Account showed securities with a book value of not far from $300,000.

Until the termination of hostilities the facilities of the Board were pledged to the Government, and all other considerations had to be subordinated to military needs. But the officers had also to keep the post-war future in mind, and the Executive Committee, at its meeting in March, 1944, authorized the appointment of a Special Advisory Committee on Research and Development, headed by President Leonard Carmichael, of Tufts College. This committee had the duty of looking into its own crystal ball and prophesying for the future. It surveyed and reconsidered the whole test program of the Board with a view to immediate and future needs; and a few weeks later, at the regular Board meeting, it arranged for an informal discussion on three important topics, all of them pertinent at the moment.

Should the Board return gradually to a full week's schedule of essay-type examinations in June? The answer from most of the institutions concerned was a not-too-emphatic "No." The sponsors of the new tests spoke rather contemptuously of "predictable examinations based on published, detailed course syllabi," asserting that they were primarily responsible for "a dictated and controlled secondary school curriculum." A few "die-hards," realizing that they were in a minority, said little, but looked back with a feeling of nostalgia to the Good Old Days before the psychologists had taken charge. In the Headmasters' Association the Old Guard was still entertainingly skeptical about the Aptitude and Achievement Tests. But the Chairman of the Board, Dean Miller, expressed the consensus of opinion when he said in a carefully phrased statement:

There seems to be a general tendency to agree that the new brief schedule is, on the whole, superior to the longer essay-type June series of the past, with some doubts expressed as to the length of time during which that superiority may exist when, to use Professor Brigham's figure, we have moved out of the framework which had been set up by the old tradition.

Would a uniform series of placement tests be useful to the Board colleges, especially for returning veterans? At the moment this problem was regarded as of "tremendous importance," and the hope was expressed that the Board might lead the way in devising tests which would take into consideration the fact that veterans had been for a long time away from textbooks and classrooms. Fortunately the situation never became very serious, and no action was necessary.

Should the service of the Board be extended to include even a larger number of outside groups and special tests for special purposes? Fear had been expressed that the development and administration of tests for groups outside the Board clientele would lead it into an entirely new field and that its original aims would be subordinated. The question of general policy was never brought to a vote, but the Executive Secretary expressed his own view by saying: "The background, knowledge, and experience in technical construction which made the Board the logical choice for the government work it has carried on makes it the logical organization to develop tests needed for educational readjustment after the war."

By common consent the Board continued to take on new outside jobs whenever they had a special appeal. For example, a joint committee of the Actuarial Society of America and the American Institute of Actuaries discussed with Professor Mullins plans whereby the Board would prepare, administer, and score tests for these societies—tests which would be chiefly concerned with mathematics and statistics on the college level. At the meeting on April 12, 1944, the Executive Secretary was authorized to proceed with this project, provided that the two societies reimburse the Board for all expenses incurred. By 1946 the Board was serving not only its member colleges and the actuarial societies but also the United States Department of State, the Bureau of Naval Personnel, the United States Naval Academy, the Coast Guard Academy, the National Administrative Board for Pepsi-Cola Scholarships, and the National Registration Office. The Executive Committee was clearly temporizing, allowing the Research Laboratories to fill any order which would pay for itself. Within only a short period the general question of policy was settled by the establishment of the Educational Testing Service.

In the spring of 1940, at the urgent request of a number of secondary schoolmen, the Board undertook the publication of a handbook containing the entrance requirements, together with related information, of all the member colleges. Dr. William A. Neilson was persuaded to serve as general editor and chairman of the committee in charge, and the first issue, appearing in February, 1941, received widespread approval. Unfortunately, because of the changes in entrance requirements brought about by the war, it became necessary to withdraw from distribution the second edition of the handbook, although it had already been set up in type. The first edition had already found its place as an essential reference book for school heads, guidance officers, and students considering what college they should attend.

In the midst of the war the Board lost several of the personages who had been most responsible for its success. Dr. Wilson Farrand, the last of the Founders except President Butler to survive, died on November 4, 1942, at the ripe age of eighty, still in his old age the same punctilious gentleman, proud of his position as Chief Custodian. Professor Carl C. Brigham, who had continued to toil unceasingly even when he knew that his doom was upon him, died on January 24, 1943, before reaching fifty, happy in the knowledge that the April tests which he had sponsored were being almost universally used. Professor Fiske, who had been living in quiet retirement since 1935, died on January 10, 1944, after his eightieth birthday, and Professor Corwin, another rugged "old-timer," died on October 14 of the same year. He delighted novices at Board meetings by explaining that certain college presidents, both male and female, were not as formidable as they looked.

President-Emeritus Neilson lived throughout the war, but died on February 13, 1946, alert and vigorous to the end. These were all men whose presence at the meetings was stimulating and who are still warmly remembered.

There were other significant changes in personnel. On July 1, 1945, John M. Stalnaker resigned as Associate Secretary of the Board to become Professor of Psychology and Dean of Students at Leland Stanford University. Mention has frequently been made in these pages of the major part which he played in the later evolution of the Board. Indefatigable, confident, and unswerving in purpose, he never spared himself and labored with infectious zeal for causes in which he had faith. To his position the Board appointed Henry Chauncey, who had served for fourteen months under Mr. Stalnaker as Associate Director of the Army-Navy Qualifying Tests and had been a member of several Board committees. He was especially valuable because of his thorough understanding of the relationship of the Board's testing program to college admission and placement. Mr. Chauncey has been a skilled diplomat, endowed with forebearance and discretion. In 1946 his title was changed to Director and Treasurer.

Professor Mullins, the *fons et origo* of so many of the Board's modern policies, had exhausted himself during the strenuous days of the war and was finding his double burden as teacher and administrator a heavy one. Not wishing to lose the benefit of his wisdom and experience, the Board, at its meeting on April 10, 1946, allowed him to retire as Executive Secretary, but insisted on his continuance as chairman of the Executive Committee.

It is difficult in "the beaten way of friendship" to express adequately the affection which his associates feel towards him as comrade and leader. Throughout the decade during which he was the very active Head, he never publicly lost his temper—although he sometimes had provocation—and he directed the Board's deliberations with consummate skill and courtesy. He has a positive genius for getting diverse personalities to work together without friction and bringing out the best that is in them. Although he perceived far in advance of many others the course which the Board was bound to take, he never boasted of his prescience or even murmured "I told you so." The Board still seeks his advice and follows his suggestions—the highest tribute it can pay him.

Every well-run organization has some trusted employee who carries on while executives come and go and is familiar with all the minor details which in the aggregate are so important. Such a person was Miss Myra McLean, who joined the staff as early as 1911 and became not only Office Manager but also the confidential secretary first to Professor Fiske and then to Professor Mullins. In her later years she was an authority on the history of the Board and could put her fingers at once on papers which nearly every one else had forgotten. She retired in 1946, leaving a gap difficult to fill.

The original Constitution had been revised more than once to meet changed conditions; and in December, 1944, a Special Committee, headed by Frank Bowles, Director of Admissions at Columbia, was appointed to draft a very much modified Constitution and By-Laws, which were approved in October, 1946. At the same time, because of the greatly increased volume of work, the members of the staff were divided into six departments, each concerned with a particular phase of the Board's services: Research, Test Construction, Statistical Analysis, Test Administration, Purchasing and Accounting, and Office Administration. The simple organization "blue-printed" by Dr. Butler had now become almost as complicated as a government bureau, and it was difficult for one man to supervise all its aspects. The operating income for the year ending September 30, 1946, was $615,098.85; the excess of income over expenditures was $57,200.58; and the Custodians' Account had grown to $310,801.79.

In the Forty-Sixth *Annual Report,* prepared by Mr. Chauncey as Acting Executive Secretary, was a paragraph which presents perfectly the viewpoint of the Board administration when the war closed.

An understanding of the philosophy underlying the Board's present program of tests for college entrance has gradually become more widespread. The sudden transition that took place in 1942 from essay examinations, each based on a definite syllabus, to objective tests which cover in so far as possible the common elements of what is taught in the various schools of the country, naturally could not be accomplished with immediate understanding on the part of all concerned. Even though there has been a steady trend for more than thirty years (since the "New Plan" examinations were introduced) to the present theory of admission examinations, some lag in understanding and appreciation was to be expected. Gradually school principals and teachers have realized that special preparation is not needed for the present examinations; that the examinations are by current indications fair to students who have attended public schools or independent schools; and that colleges, in considering candidates, do not base their decisions entirely on the test scores but take into account also the school record, the recommendation of the principal and teachers, and frequently also observations from an interview.

Many provocative ideas were in the air during the months following the cessation of war activities. Some educational leaders undoubtedly wanted to return to the procedures of earlier days; others wished to push further the philosophy which had come to dominate the Board; and many were undecided, waiting for the dust to settle. Eventually the stronger, more imaginative minds seized control and brought about a new metamorphosis.

CHAPTER VIII

THE LATEST
PHASE

THE SUDDEN IMPACT of the Second World War, as we have seen, brought almost over night an unprecedented broadening of the Board's activities, chiefly to meet the needs of various branches of the armed forces, and made it resemble a manufacturing plant—which indeed it was, turning out tests as factories produced machine tools and cartridges and canned salmon. The Board's office force at 117th Street dwindled to almost zero, but the laboratories in Princeton, formerly serene and orderly, now echoed to "the busy hum of men." At meetings of the Executive Committee the members listened with astonishment to the descriptions of Professor Stalnaker's novel enterprises, wondering what could possibly be disclosed next. The research workers, in a mood of professional elation, welcomed each opportunity to extend and amplify their experiments.

Dr. Harold O. Gulliksen, Associate Professor at the University of Chicago, who joined the Board in 1942 to direct a secret project for the Office of Scientific Research and Development, was a refreshing stimulus because of his realistic approach to emergency problems. Princeton soon appointed him as Professor of Psychology, and in 1945 he accepted also the position of Research Secretary for the Board—a position which Professor Brigham had at one time occupied. Even after Hiroshima and the Japanese collapse, the volume of orders did not diminish, and Dr. Gulliksen was kept busy recruiting competent personnel. In 1945–46 the number of employees receiving monthly salaries increased from 69 to more than 100. In addition, temporary employees on hourly rates of pay worked steadily throughout the year; still another group were engaged for several months at a time during rush seasons; and others were called in during the peak scoring periods. It was reported in April, 1946, that more than 325 temporary employees (excluding Examiners, Readers, and Supervisors) were on duty at least part of that month, and a year later the figure had grown to 435. Facing an acute housing shortage for its staff, the Board purchased in 1947 an apartment building at 10 Bayard Lane, in Princeton. The laboratories, while not often visited by the average Board member, were dominating its activities and accumulating a huge reservoir of stored statistics regarding human intelligence. There was, indeed, some danger that the tail would wag the dog. With unconscious naïveté the *Report* for 1947 said: "The Board continues to maintain its New York office as a center for Board and committee meetings. Much of the editorial work on various publications is done here, and the office itself serves as a source of information about Board activities."

It is unnecessary to itemize here all the commissions to which the Research Department was pledged and for which it was being paid. For the Navy alone it completed the following: a series of seven manuals of performance and identification tests in Basic Engineering; reports of Radio-Man tests developed through its assistance; a study of Electrician's Mates tests; a study of Gunner's Mates tests; and an investigation of German naval selection methods. In addition, surveys were made of officer-like qualities and performance skills of cadets in the Coast Guard Academy and of the validity of selection methods in the Navy V-12 College Training Program. An attempt was also made to validate the tests used at the Naval Academy. These samples chosen at random will show the highly technical nature of the services which the Office of Scientific Research and Development was supplying. It was not only a producer of all types of intelligence and aptitude tests—probably the best in the world in that limited field—but also a headquarters where expert advice on these matters could be obtained.

While this amazing expansion was taking place, the Board could not ignore the purpose for which it was founded; and the number registering at the regular quarterly series for admission to college had grown steadily, from 26,166 in 1943–44 to 32,589 in 1944–45 and 46,087 in 1945–46. Commenting on this trend, the Secretary wrote in 1946:

It appears that a substantial number of colleges are now, for the first time, either requiring all candidates to take the Board's tests or more strongly recommending that these tests be taken. The increased use of the Board's tests is probably an outcome of several tendencies and circumstances: first, an increased number of applicants due largely to reduced military needs; second, a growing realization of the need for standardized evidence regarding each college applicant and

a growing confidence in the value of the Board's tests for
that purpose; and third, a growing recognition of the efficiency and economy of a centralized system of college entrance examinations such as the Board maintains.

In numbers that year the University of Pennsylvania
led the list with 2,159 candidates, followed by Cornell
with 2,109 and Yale with 2,107. Wellesley was at the
top of the women's colleges, with 1,486. Scores for the
1945–46 series were reported to 385 colleges and universities, of whom only 53 were then members of the
Board. Clearly, what the Board had to offer was being
appreciated by institutions which in the prewar days
had manifested little interest in it. Its work for the
Federal Government had advertised it in every corner
of the land.

The Research Department took a justifiable pride
in performing unusual services for both member and
nonmember colleges. In response to a general request,
it prepared placement examinations in French, German, Latin, Spanish, Biology, Chemistry, and Physics.
Through 1946 it administered a Special Aptitude Test
for veterans, twice a month in nine cities for an aggregate of 4,471 "G.I.'s." It even evolved a test of Reading
Comprehension and an examination in English for
foreign students. The Executive Secretary declared in
1946, "The Board could readily prepare tests in other
fields in which there is an indication of interest on the
part of several institutions." As it was then set up, the
Board was equipped to meet any legitimate demand,
as a factory weaves many different types of fabric to
order.

The year 1946 saw one marked change in policy—in

some respects a reversion to an earlier procedure. For several years a practice booklet had been distributed in advance to all students registered for the Scholastic Aptitude Test. A further step had been to provide practice questions for all those taking the Comprehensive Mathematics Tests. Now the Board decided that typical items from each of the Achievement Tests should also be made available to the candidates. The psychologists had hitherto opposed such action on the ground that it would encourage "cramming" for the examinations. The justification for the publication of sample questions was mainly that they minimized the element of surprise and reduced the danger of misunderstanding directions during the excitement of the examination period. This concession to the conservatives was much appreciated by some schools and teachers who had never lost their faith in concentrated preparation for examinations.

The Achievement Tests used in the 1940's included English Composition, Social Studies, Spatial Relations, Chemistry, Physics, Biology, and Reading Examinations in six languages—French, German, Spanish, Latin, Greek, and Italian. In this series undoubtedly the most controversial item was the English Composition—the *bête noir* of the Research Department, which regarded it scornfully as an anachronism; indeed, it had been publicly proclaimed that "the problems involved in developing a reliable essay examination are, if not unsolvable, at least far from solved at the present time." The chief cause alleged for the unreliability of the reading was "the difficulty of keeping thirty to seventy-five teachers 'in tune' with their grading." The scientific experts, regarding the essay-type of examination as a demonstration of the inadequacy and inaccuracy of human judgments as contrasted with the efficiency of mechanical checking, could not be expected to be enthusiastic about it. On the other hand, many excellent English instructors, while recognizing its imperfections, saw in it values to which psychologists were blind. One member of a school English Department growled, "These scientists want to dehumanize their own language and leave it nothing but symbols." The issue was clearly drawn, and has never definitely been settled.

The popular Chairman of the Board after 1946 was Professor Edward S. Noyes, Associate Professor of English and Chairman of the Board of Admissions at Yale University. A graduate of Yale in the Class of 1913, Professor Noyes later earned his Master's and Doctor's degrees at the same institution. After having served his apprenticeship as one of the Board's Readers in English, he succeeded Professor Jack R. Crawford, also of Yale, as Chief Reader in 1936, the date when Professor Mullins became Executive Secretary and so many momentous changes in the Board organization were effected. As Chief Reader in English, he won the co-operation of his very diverse and sometimes stubborn associates; and he performed the same function as Chairman of the Board, guiding it through a very critical period when he had to make and ratify many vital decisions. With balanced judgment and discreet manner, he kept the pendulum from swinging too far away from a stable center and curbed its speed when it approached recklessness. He was the ideal man to be in charge while the Board, for what it thought to be the public good, committed a notable act of renunciation and self-decapitation.

A Great Change was indeed, in the offing. As far back as 1937 Professor Mullins, whose imagination usually outstripped contemporary thinking, had suggested informally to Dr. William S. Learned, of the Carnegie Foundation for the Advancement of Teaching, that it might be possible for several of the major nonprofit testing organizations to work together towards common aims; both men later prepared memorandums outlining their views regarding co-ordination or consolidation. In April, 1937, without any publicity, the Executive Committee authorized the appointment of an Advisory Committee to confer with the Executive Secretary "on ways and means of increasing the services of the Board." The members included Dean Heermance (chairman), President Ferry, Dr. Fuess, President Neilson, Professor Noyes, President Marion E. Park, and Dr. Gummere (*ex officio*).

It was soon apparent that there were sharp differences of opinion regarding the usefulness of the Board and the need for some new organization. Critics spoke of the Board as "narrow and provincial" and complained of the "ultra-conservative nature of its clientele." Mr. Stalnaker, on the other hand, felt that the Board might conceivably swallow up or absorb several of the less well-endowed organizations. Dr. Jessup, of the Carnegie Foundation, intimated that it might be interested in helping the Board financially "if its services could be expanded in certain directions." Dr. Learned was evidently thinking in terms of a new "general examination board."

Professor Brigham, although he was convalescing from an illness, prepared and sent to the Advisory Committee in October, 1947, a long memorandum entitled, "The Place of Research in a Testing Organization," presenting his personal viewpoint "on the possible hazards to education in setting up any organization to perpetuate the present types of tests and the possible advantages to education in setting up an organization which sponsors investigation and research and constantly revises its testing practices to conform with the results of the research."

At the October meeting of the Board Professor Mullins brought to the attention of the Advisory Committee Dr. Learned's proposal for the merging of the existing agencies. This was favorably discussed by President Conant at the conference of the Educational Records Bureau in December. Meanwhile the Advisory Committee had appointed a subcommittee consisting of President Neilson, Miss Park, and Dr. Fuess to draft a tentative report on all the matters involved. This was ready before the close of the year and, in brief, advocated that the Board join with four other agencies "in making a frontal attack on problems pertaining to testing and examination." It was suggested that more enduring progress could be achieved if a research program could be subsidized for a five-year period by a grant of $50,000 —presumably from the Carnegie Corporation—and that meanwhile the College Entrance Examination Board would remain autonomous and continue its usual services and functions. This report of the subcommittee was later adopted by the Advisory Committee, with only slight verbal modifications.

Professor Brigham, speaking for himself and not for the Board, called Learned's idea a "destructive move." It soon became clear that no subsidy would be forthcoming, and it was quietly agreed that the subject should be dropped. It was never discussed at a full meeting of the Board, and no mention of it was made by Professor Mullins in his *Report* for 1938. Some of the details did leak out, however, and there was gossip about them at luncheons and dinners. At the moment sentiment was rather strong against the Board's giving up any of its identity. Furthermore, there were symptoms of distrust on both sides which could not be ignored. Professor Mullins handled the negotiations with his native and mollifying tact, restraining the participants when they showed signs of getting out of hand and yet insisting on free discussion. The advent of war put an end to any possibility of immediate amalgamation.

The rapid expansion of testing services after 1941 set people thinking. Early in 1946 representatives of the Carnegie Foundation for the Advancement of Teaching and the Carnegie Corporation opened up the subject again with certain officers of the Board; and in October, the Carnegie Foundation's Committee on Testing, headed by President Conant, recommended a consolidation of the various groups then engaged in the preparation and administration of tests. They emphasized the overlapping, duplication, and consequent waste because several agencies, with similar objectives and the same general scope, were operating, to some extent competitively, in the same field. According to the committee there was a crying need for "the creation of a single testing agency which could unify, strengthen, and expand the present testing functions of the nonprofit agencies, sponsor distinguished research both on existing tests and on unexplored test areas, and generally make available tests of the highest standards." Why not merge and share the cost and the glory?

It is always difficult to fix the precise moment when fruitful ideas are sown or germinate. Important changes may develop out of mere hints or casual "around-the-fire" conversations, which spread faster and farther than their author intended. In this case, after the initial suggestion had been dropped, people began to take sides, and by the time the Board assembled for its fall meeting everybody was talking and reacting in accordance with their thought patterns. Opinions ranged from ill-concealed surprise and shock to demonstrative enthusiasm. The "in-betweeners" were willing to listen and be shown.

The Report of the Carnegie Committee, while not entirely unexpected at Board headquarters, caused no small amount of excitement among the Board members. There was no doubt in the minds of those who had considered the matter carefully that the proposal had merit. On the other hand, it was essential that the interests of the Board, and especially of its widening constituency, should be protected. Furthermore, it was not pleasant for some of the responsible leaders to contemplate the abandonment of a function which, by common consent, had been so well performed. Of the testing agencies, the Board presumably had the most to lose, both in actual cash contribution and in prestige.

At the October meeting President Conant, President Edmund E. Day, of Cornell, and President Henry M.

Wriston, of Brown—three very persuasive speakers— appeared by invitation to explain the motives and expectations of the Carnegie Committee. It was clear after their addresses that, while there was a majority agreement as to the values to be attained by such a merger, opposition had developed as to the form of organization outlined. From trios and quartettes in the corners and corridors could be heard the comments: "If we do this, we might as well fold up"; "Why, by this plan the Board loses its identity"; "Aren't we getting along all right as it is?" If a vote had been insisted on then and there, the plan would doubtless have been rejected.

It was wisely decided, however, to ask a special group "to consider the place of the Board in the field of testing, with special reference to the report of the Carnegie Committee." This important body was headed by Katharine McBride, who had been President of Bryn Mawr College since 1942. Since her field was Education and Psychology, she was exceptionally well qualified to pass on the considerations involved. With her were President Bancroft Beatley, of Simmons, President Everett N. Case, of Colgate, Lester Nelson, Principal of the Scarsdale High School, Frank D. Ashburn, of the Brooks School, Professor Noyes, and Professor Mullins. With the exception of the last two, who served *ex officio*, the group was made up of what might be called "new blood," representative of a younger educational generation. The Board, as so often in its history, was looking forward to the future and what it might bring.

Any glance back would have shown that the Board, partly through the accident of war, had wandered far beyond its original boundaries. As the penalty of efficiency, it was now engaged in a score of projects, and in so doing had trespassed on areas already pre-empted by other organizations. The special committee realized the stock arguments for a controlled non-profit monopoly; yet it also had the responsibility of preserving the Board's autonomy and financial independence and its admission testing program.

With these points in mind, the special committee prepared a report outlining the considerations to be used as a basis for negotiations with the other interested testing agencies—in particular the American Council on Education and the Carnegie Foundation for the Advancement of Teaching. Conferences and discussions took place during the spring and summer. Difficulties were gradually ironed out, and criticisms answered. Eventually a so-called "Agreement" was drafted, reasonably satisfactory to all the parties concerned, and at the fall meeting of the Board in 1947 it was adopted with no dissenting voice.

In brief, the Agreement provided for the formation of a completely new organization to be called the Educational Testing Service—usually shortened to ETS— a nonprofit, nonstock corporation without members, administered by a board of ten trustees, of whom four were to be named by the College Entrance Examination Board. To the foundation of the ETS the Board was to contribute all its assets in excess of $300,000, the Carnegie Corporation was to furnish $750,000 in cash and securities, and the American Council was to give "all of its assets in connection with its testing activities in excess of $185,000." Thus the ETS would start with ample resources in the way of endowment.

What the Board was doing was voluntarily to abandon all its "outside activities," including its laboratories and research staff, and to limit its attention to problems connected with the transition from school to college, and in particular to the admissions testing program. It was to continue to prescribe the tests to be included, set the examination dates and fees, appoint the examining committee in each subject, and generally specify the procedures to be followed in the construction, administration, scoring, and reporting. In turning over its operating facilities to the Educational Testing Service, the Board did so "in the belief and in the confidence" that the ETS "would make good tests more widely available, set standards of good tests against which those of other agencies would be judged, increase research in the area of testing, and accelerate the development of new types of tests." In agreeing to the merger the Board was influenced by motives entirely altruistic and had nothing whatever to gain for itself and its members except the possibility of better testing services for everybody.

The projects now to be relinquished by the Board had during the year 1946–47 required financial expenditures amounting to more than one-third of its total budget; and nearly every member of the Board's staff had devoted part of his time to some phase of what were called "the non-traditional testing programs." About 65,000 candidates presented themselves for one or more of the routine college entrance examinations during the same period; but beyond this, almost 40,000 high school Seniors had taken the Pepsi-Cola Scholarship Test on one day, not to mention 42,000 candidates for the Navy Aptitude Test and several thousand young men who were tested for other purposes, including entrance to the Military, Naval, and Coast Guard academies, the Foreign Service, or the actuarial profession. As the Director said, "One testing program or special project has been followed almost immediately by another." All these ventures were now to be transferred to the Educational Testing Service.

The Educational Testing Service actually came into legal existence on December 19, 1947, when it was granted a charter under the Education Law of the State of New York. On January 1, 1948, by advance agreement, the plan of merger became effective, and the ETS began operation. Some weeks earlier the Board had turned over to the ETS its laboratories, its equipment, and all its tangible assets except the New York office on West 117th Street, with its lease and furniture. On and as of December 31, 1947, the Custodians contributed to the ETS securities with a market value of $246,472.50. At the same time the Board transferred all its contracts and agreements for test development, construction, administration, and research, not directly connected with its college entrance examinations. The Board had already made a contract with the ETS, effective at the beginning of the new year, by the terms of which the responsibility for preparation, distribution, administration, scoring, and reporting of the usual college admission tests and for administrative and developmental work connected therewith was assumed by ETS for a term of five years. In other words, the Board was to use the ETS as its testing agent and pay it for services rendered.

The new Educational Testing Service was governed

by a Board of Trustees, consisting initially of the president of the American Council on Education, George F. Zook, the chairman of the College Entrance Examination Board, Edward S. Noyes, and the president of the Carnegie Foundation for the Advancement of Teaching, Oliver C. Carmichael, together with nine others, three appointed by each of the *ex officio* members. These included President Raymond Allen, of the University of Washington, President Joseph W. Barker, of the Research Corporation in New York City, President James B. Conant, of Harvard University, Senator James W. Fulbright, of Arkansas, Superintendent Harold Hunt, of the Chicago Public Schools, President Katharine McBride, of Bryn Mawr College, Dean Thomas R. McConnell, of the University of Minnesota, Principal Lester E. Nelson, of Scarsdale High School, and Commissioner Frank T. Spaulding, of New York. At the first meeting, on December 20, 1947, President Conant was elected chairman of the Board of Trustees and Mr. Barker, chairman of the Executive Committee. Henry Chauncey, Director of the College Entrance Examination Board, was appointed president of the Educational Testing Service.

No bell-ringing or flag-raising announced the opening of the Educational Testing Service, and visitors to Princeton in January saw substantially the same set-up that had existed in December. As a matter of fact, most of the Board's personnel were doing their jobs in the same buildings for another equally benevolent employer. Professor Gulliksen, the Research Director, together with Richard H. Sullivan, the Assistant Director, and William W. Turnbull, the Secretary, all submitted their resignations to the Board at the meeting in April, 1948, and all three continued without intermission in their work at Princeton under the ETS.

In an announcement sent out on December 29, 1947, the ETS said: "The Trustees are firmly committed to interfere in no way with the non-testing activities of the organizations which have brought the ETS into being." Their more positive policy was expressed in the following sentences:

The Trustees will rather be concerned with developing new services and new tests in areas where they are badly needed, with conducting research in areas in which no fundamental work is being done, and with providing a type of counselling service which hitherto has been unavailable except to limited groups. They will hope to stimulate research and sound testing procedures everywhere and to help educators who feel a need for guidance in the selection, use, and interpretation of tests.

To this ideal the ETS has remained loyal, and the relations between it and the Board have been uniformly friendly. Even those who once were not well disposed towards the merger—or, as it has also been called, the divorce—have good reason to feel that the step was a wise one for both the Board and for American education in general.

Throughout this confusing transition period, very fortunately, Professor Noyes remained as chairman of the Board and Professor Mullins as chairman of the Executive Committee, and they managed diplomatically the details of the various necessary arrangements. Further continuity for the Board was preserved by the appointment of an interim committee consisting of

Frank H. Bowles, Director of Admissions at Columbia University (chairman), Mrs. Dorothy B. Osborne, headmistress of the Spence School, and Dean Samuel T. Arnold, of Brown University. These carried on the routine administration until July 31, 1948. On August 1, by appointment of the Executive Committee, Mr. Bowles became Director, and shortly afterwards he was joined by William C. Fels, as Secretary. Mr. Bowles thus became the latest in the succession of able men who have sustained the burden of the Board.

Once determined upon, the "great change" which some of the officers had dreaded was accomplished with a minimum of friction. The members continued to use the Board as they always had done, and many of them felt relief at returning to the modest organization with which they were familiar and to budgets which did not involve such vast sums of money. Things were, perhaps, less exciting, but more within their range of comprehension. The New York offices had to be refurnished and rearranged. The Board was now a purchaser, instead of a producer of tests; and the first report from the ETS of the cost of operations for the Board account indicated that the inflationary trend was affecting even the making of examinations. Accordingly the Board increased its fees by one dollar for each test program or two dollars for the combined series—thus following the practice, not uncommon in industry, of passing increased costs on to the consumer.

At the close of nine months of operation under the new system, the Director voiced his conclusions as follows:

It is a pleasure to report that to date the terms of the agreement and the relationships under it have been thoroughly satisfactory. The technical services of the Testing Service have been, at all times, fully available to the Board and, more important than these services, the wisdom, experience, and good will of the officers of the Testing Service have been a reserve fund upon which the officers of the Board have drawn freely.

The effect of the merger, in so far as it can be assessed to date, has been to free the Board of the responsibility for administering large and diverse testing programs in the areas other than college testing while, at the same time, making thoughtful provision for the continuance of such programs under an organization maintained for the purpose and happily skilled in its work. So far as the Board's operations are concerned, the freedom that its officers and committees enjoy in the planning and control of Board work is beyond price. The problems of college entrance testing, although explored systematically for fifty years, are not solved, and in a developing culture such as ours can never be solved. Nevertheless, the concentration of effort that the Board is now enabled to make should make possible the discovery of some answers that we do not now know.

Paradoxically, as the scope of the Board's activities narrowed, its college clientage broadened. The new Director, commenting on this trend, said:

The entire country is gradually becoming the Board's stage. Although the membership is still predominantly eastern, the steady and rapid addition of colleges from the Middle West, South, and Far West augurs a day not far off when the Board will be truly representative of the entire country.

In February, 1947, Mr. Bowles made a reconnoitering tour of the western colleges, as a direct consequence of which the Board voted in April to establish a branch on the Pacific Coast. Dr. A. Glenwood Walker accepted the position as its head and was installed in October 1 in an office in Berkeley, California, The number of strictly college entrance candidates meanwhile continued to increase, reaching for 1947–48 the stupendous total of 75,158—a growth of 42 percent in two years. In 1947 alone seventeen new institutions joined the Board, including Boston University, Oberlin, Pomona, and Notre Dame; and under its revised constitution several secondary school associations became full members of the Board, with one to five voting representatives. The Director had to remind the members that the meetings were so well attended that they might not be conducive to the intimate discussion of educational problems and that it might, therefore, be desirable to hold concurrently with the semiannual gatherings of the Board smaller conferences on topics of current interest to selected groups of educators.

As a phase of this thrilling postwar renaissance, several of the Board's publications were revised or revived. During the 1930's a brief *News Bulletin* had been sent out intermittently to the Board's patrons, but it had lapsed in the turmoil of the 1940's. In the spring of 1947, however, it reappeared as *The College Board Review: News and Research of the College Entrance Examination Board,* under the editorship of Dr. Herbert S. Conrad, of the Princeton Laboratory group, and about 12,000 copies were distributed. Dr. Conrad continued this project after the Educational Testing Service was created, but in November, 1948, it was taken over by the Board and has since been edited by the Secretary, Mr. Fels.

In December, 1946, all students inquiring about tests were sent a 32-page pamphlet called *Bulletin of Information,* and each candidate was presented with a copy before registering for the particular combination of tests appropriate to his preparation and his needs. The number of copies distributed has been well over 150,000 a year. Since every candidate receives this *Bulletin,* there can be no discrimination. Everybody has an equal chance to study the samples and become familiar with the type of test he has to face.

A third edition of the *Annual Handbook, Terms of Admission to the Colleges of the College Entrance Examination Board,* which had been first compiled by Dr. Neilson and later continued under the editorship of Dr. Ada Comstock Notestein, was ready early in 1947. The fourth edition, published in 1948, included ninety-three out of a possible ninety-four of the institutions which were either members or expected to become members, and was sent out without cost to schools making any significant use of the Board's examinations. In commenting on its usefulness, the Director intimated that it made "a dull business of the important work of the choice of a college." This was certainly true. But it must be added, in all fairness, that the statements were prepared by the college officials and if they were unalluring, Dr. Notestein was surely not to blame.

As the Board, after its divagations, resumed again its main-traveled road, Mr. Bowles undertook to elucidate once more the philosophy of its modern tests. His attitude, and that of the Board, are best revealed through direct quotation.

In conferences, in publications, and perhaps even in films, it should be possible to make clear to college and school men, and to candidates and their parents, the nature and purpose of the Board's program. For though the present test series is now in its seventh year, there are many people who do not understand fully the guiding principles on which the tests are based. There is still confusion between the present program and the essay examinations used prior to 1942. Parents in particular are ignorant of the nature of the present tests because they last took an interest in the Board at the time when they themselves were applying for admission to college. An explanatory film that could be shown to parent-teacher associations and to other interested groups might be effective in presenting the new points of view.

It is hard, for example, for parents to believe that cramming is no longer necessary, that the tests are to be taken in stride, that considerable latitude in the content of courses and the method of teaching is possible without handicapping students, that the tests are equally fair to candidates from public and private schools, that the objective tests with their large number of items and wide sampling of subject matter provide an "album of candid shots" as compared with the "eight or ten posed photographs" of the former essay examinations, that there is no passing mark, and that each college applies its own standards and considers the test results not by themselves but along with the school record, principal's report, interview estimate, and all the other information available. These concepts or principles need to be disseminated widely, not only to give peace of mind to teachers, students, and parents, but also to enable the schools, in formulating their educational program, to take advantage of the freedom permitted by the new tests.

I doubt whether anywhere in print can be found a clearer, more accurate, and more sympathetic summary of what its proponents claimed for the new program. The tests were never allowed to become static or inflexible. When some teachers noticed that the Verbal Section of the Scholastic Aptitude Test had not been altered for some years, there was a temptation for them to revert to the old-fashioned direct preparation, through vocabulary drill and similar techniques, for this section of the examination. The situation obviously encouraged "cramming"; and accordingly, in April, 1947, the Examiners unexpectedly introduced a Verbal Section differing markedly from its immediate predecessors, with a sharp reduction in the number of antonym questions. I can recall well the expression on the face of one instructor who discovered that all his coaching had gone for naught. "Confound it!" he cried, "You can never tell what those fellows down at Princeton are going to do next!" And you never could.

As the Board approached its semicentennial, it was still the English Composition test which caused the most complaint. Those concerned with costs did not like it because it consumed almost $50,000 a year—an amount approximately double the Board's total expenditure for research in 1946. The Research Department in desperation tried one experiment after another, finally in 1947 giving a test which included in one paper all three kinds of recognized test material—objective, traditional essay, and paragraph revision. An impartial survey of results showed that for correlation purposes the objective section rated first, the theme second, and paragraph revision definitely last. On the basis of statistics the Research Department asserted that the objective type of question was more useful as a measuring technique than either of the other two. But the many English teachers who still had a fondness for the essay were not to be silenced by mathematical arguments. The Director, in summarizing the perennial controversy, said: "The debate is an important one for the Board. A considerable weight of opinion is on the side of the essay tests, whereas the weight of present evidence appears to lie more heavily on the side of the objective material."

In 1948, when the theme question was deliberately omitted from two of the four series, the resentment in some quarters was bitter. Mr. Bowles once again pointed out the Board's dilemma:

The facts concerning reading and scoring costs on the one hand and the predictive value of theme questions on the other, constitute an impressive support of a strictly objective form of test. The arguments of these advocates are persuasive, but they have not yet downed the nagging conviction that, in English Composition, the whole is more than the sum of its parts. If there were a reasonable chance of isolating, as factors subject to objective testing and objective judgment, *all* of the parts, and if there were an agreement that the whole was equal to the sum of its parts, then there would be conclusive argument for objective testing. However, until such isolation has been completed, and such agreement has been reached, the Board is obliged to consider the possibility of testing ability to write English by having the candidate write English.

There the matter rests—or to be more explicit, the controversy goes merrily on, with neither faction willing to yield. And the dispute is not likely to be over for some time to come.

By this period the attendance at the semi-annual meetings had grown so large that it seemed best to transfer them from the dignified Trustees' Room in the old Columbia Library to an assembly hall in the Biltmore Hotel, more easily accessible to the delegates than the room on Morningside Heights, but not nearly so distinctive. The less youthful members have pleasant memories of the portraits, the dark woodwork, the high ceilings, and the view as they walked out of the building from the stone steps down across 116th Street to the tennis courts and beyond. That massive room must be haunted by the spirits of a bygone day: Professor Fiske, white-haired, deliberate, and sonorous of speech; President Neilson, brisk, whimsical, and provocative; Miss Woolley, exemplifying the creed which she once expressed in the exclamation, "How uncomfortable to be a static female in a world where all the males are moving!"; Professor Corwin, with his vigilant energy; Dr. Farrand, a perpetual fountain of scholastic lore; Professor Brigham, meeting criticism with an expert's tolerant air; and the nuns in their black and white, anonymous and silent, but adding their bit of picturesqueness to the gathering.

In the new surroundings something of the homelike atmosphere has disappeared, together with the suggestion of Victorianism. But even in modern conventional hotel quarters, the Board is still an intimate body. Nobody seems unduly worried or hurried; greetings are exchanged between friends who have not seen one another for months; new members are congratulated and introduced to the "old-timers"; animated discussions occasionally break out on the floor. It is all very simple and uninhibited. Here one cannot help feeling that the Board is better off for returning to its original mission. It lost something during the war, when it was more complex and mechanical.

The streamlining of the modern Board was symbolized in the format of the 48th *Annual Report*. The former plain brown cover was replaced by a light gray with white lettering—more appealing than the older booklet. The change was significant, an intentional break with the past. But the attentive reader will observe that only the cover has been radically altered. The problems dealt with in the text are much the same, and the same committees are evidently dealing with the familiar problems. Perhaps this indicates what has happened. The Board has in some respects adjusted itself to new conditions, but the aims and procedures are basically what they always were.

Professor Noyes had guided the Board through its critical period of deflation and retired at the fall meeting in 1949, with honor. To his position as Chairman the Board elected Katharine E. McBride, President of Bryn Mawr College. A graduate of Bryn Mawr, Miss McBride had later taken her doctorate there in Psychology, had become a professor, and after two years as Dean of Radcliffe College, had succeeded Miss Park as President of Bryn Mawr. A charter Trustee of the Educational Testing Service, she is, of course, thoroughly acquainted with testing, in theory and in practice. The members of the Board have learned to respect her scholarly mind, her insistence on high standards, her fairness in discussion, and they are not unaware that these are accompanied by feminine charm and grace. Nobody could be better qualified to start the Board on a new and prosperous era.

The death of President Butler on December 7, 1947, removed the last living person who had participated in the creation of the College Entrance Board. A few months before his death, when he was incapacitated by almost total blindness, he wrote Chairman Noyes:

It is a half century since I brought this Board into existence, and when I recall the chaotic conditions relative to everything regarding college entrance in this country at that time, I realize as probably no one else can the enormous service which the Board has rendered. I am sure it will continue to render like service in whatever policies it decides to adopt.

The child of Butler's conception had, indeed, had a strange, eventful history. Quickly passing through adolescence to maturity, it had suffered attacks of illness when its demise seemed imminent, but had then made its own diagnosis, prescribed its own curatives, and recovered its health, to go on to even more remarkable accomplishments. Then, after extending its activities into allied fields and winning new laurels, it turned over of its own volition much of its newly acquired responsibility to another agency, and, not without relief, abandoned its dreams of magnitude. It is content with knowing that during its first half century it probably achieved more in the scientific development of examinations than any other organization.

It has, indeed, done a great work, but its work will never really be done. More and more, as experts peer into the secret recesses of the human mind, new methods of investigation and analysis and prediction will be discovered. Already the ideas of 1900 seem obsolete; and the time will undoubtedly arrive when much of what the Board proudly regards as good will be discarded. But the Board in crises has shown an amazing gift for adjustment to changed conditions; and if its arteries do not harden, if it does not lose this flexibility, there is no reason why it should not reach its centenary still experimenting and still asking, with Pontius Pilate, "What is truth?" Its job is certainly not finished, and the enticing vistas that lie ahead encourage it to go forward with faith and hope.

CHAPTER IX

WHAT
LIES
AHEAD?

As the College Entrance Examination Board nears its fiftieth birthday no signs of premature decrepitude are evident. Those who feared that its usefulness might be weakened when it helped to create the Educational Testing Service were needlessly alarmed. Indeed, it now seems to move with greater ease, like a traveler who has unburdened himself of a heavy load. The current problems are fascinating, engrossing enough to keep the Director and his associates profitably occupied. Recent meetings have attracted some of the most influential of contemporary school and college leaders.

The Board is still, of course, the creature of the colleges that support it, and these have recently become more numerous and heterogeneous. During its early history it was composed of a small group of eastern colleges with a common purpose and much the same outlook. Indeed, its active support came from a very few colleges and universities, whose admissions officers knew one another intimately. Lately, however, the membership has included institutions with interests and philosophies different from those of the original sponsors—

although no doubt equally commendable. Some of the great universities, such as Ohio State, Minnesota, Wisconsin, and Iowa, have never joined, but the membership extends from Bowdoin on the Northeast Coast to California on the Pacific. The institutions admitted in 1948 included the University of Massachusetts and the University of Virginia, Western Reserve University and Manhattanville College of the Sacred Heart.

This diversity may mean, as the Director has suggested, "that the Board operations will come to represent compromises of the diverging interests of a number of institutions rather than a single policy arrived at by the full consent of a few institutions." No longer will Harvard, Yale, and Princeton, supported by the Seven Women's Colleges, dominate the thinking of the Board as they so often have done in the past. If the trend continues, the relatively simple structure of Professor Fiske will have to broaden its base and add new compartments to accommodate the varied needs of a hundred different institutions. Many of the Board's early leaders had visions of a thoroughly national body, and their dreams seem now on the verge of realization. Possibly the Board has been at times too provincial, its outlook too limited. Certainly it has learned much in the testing field from scholars at Chicago, Iowa, and Leland Stanford. Its recent spread to the West and the South, while it may frighten a few timid Casper Milquetoasts, should avert smugness and isolation.

The Director has pointed out with praiseworthy candor, that there is a noticeable reaction among secondary schoolmasters and college professors in favor of examinations based on set requirements. Some sensitive observers have long felt that the educational psychologists, while fundamentally right, had insisted on carrying their formula too far. Mr. Bowles has admitted that "the Board's action in moving away from definitions of subject matter fields is now being questioned both at secondary school and college levels." In matters of this kind it is natural for research workers to ride a theory too hard and claim too much. At any rate, the situation needs a thorough investigation—and this, in the present mood of the Board, it is bound to have.

Even the most credulous scientist would hardly maintain that finality has been reached in the delicate business of testing. The matter of aural tests in the modern foreign languages has never been fully explored. Many history teachers are still dissatisfied with the Achievement Test in the so-called "Social Studies." Other skeptics question the validity of the picturesque test in Spatial Relations. And there is always, when the committee room becomes too placid, the controversial English Composition examination to consider. College admissions officers are agreed that they have today far more accurate and helpful information regarding the qualifications of applicants, but they are not so unanimous regarding the value of all the tests that are offered. The spread of the junior college, with the inevitable desire of some of its graduates to transfer later to senior colleges, have made it desirable to provide tests evaluating its work. There has occasionally been a cry from the secondary schools for terminal examinations which can be used as checks on their teachers and teaching. Finally, the needs of the more than ten thousand candidates who now each year take the Board examinations as preliminary candidates have not been fully met.

Whether or not the Board can reach and preserve unanimity on these technical matters, it has succeeded, and is succeeding, in its aim of bringing the colleges and schools closer together. There are those who feel that the Board, if so disposed, could be a more potent influence in setting standards; but this can be accomplished only if its membership is agreed on what those standards should be. The age-old battle between the humanists and the vocationalists makes it probable that agreement cannot be expected. But the fact that specialists on various levels of education can meet at least twice a year and renew their acquaintance as well as their discussions is good for everybody concerned. Complete uniformity in education in the United States is neither possible nor desirable. Competent teachers will continue to seek the same ends through different routes and may even follow the same route to different ends. The essential thing for the Board is to be open-minded and alert. Mr. Bowles showed his quality as Director when he wrote in 1948:

As a static organization resting on its present program and operations, the Board would surely become archaic and outmoded with the first major change in either college or secondary school curricula. Indeed, there is evidence that, in the past, the Board on at least one occasion came perilously near to outliving its then usefulness by reason of such changes.

As it celebrates the close of its first half century, the Board has a comfortable backlog of endowment and enjoys the confidence of its patrons. It provides a convenient forum where various theories can be advocated and debated. Its record is creditable; its leadership is intelligent; its ideals are high. It is with courage and optimism that it opens the door to tomorrow.

INDEX